westermann

D1718170

Pathway
Advanced

Prep Course

Lese- und Arbeitsbuch zur Vorbereitung auf die gymnasiale Oberstufe

Herausgegeben und erarbeitet von:
Iris Edelbrock

Sprachliche Betreuung:
John Poziemski

westermann GRUPPE

© 2020 Bildungshaus Schulbuchverlage
Westermann Schroedel Diesterweg Schöningh Winklers GmbH, Braunschweig
www.westermann.de

Druck A[1] / Jahr 2020
Alle Drucke der Serie A sind im Unterricht parallel verwendbar.

Redaktion: Marion Kramer
Umschlaggestaltung: Nora Krull; Fotos: Rubens Alarcon/Alamy Stock Foto (vorn);
ocean_nikonos/stock.adobe.com (hinten)
Druck und Bindung: Westermann Druck GmbH, Braunschweig

ISBN 978-3-14-**040217**-0

Contents

Level of difficulty	Webcodes
●○○ basic ●●○ intermediate ●●● advanced	All **audio**, **audio-visual material** and **worksheets** are provided on web-codes. Access the following website www.westermann.de/webcode and enter the respective code.

COMPREHENSION

Making a Difference: The Beginning of Change?

ANALYSIS

Growing Up – No Longer Being a Child!

East, West, Home's Best? – Culture & Identity

Lernen und Arbeiten mit dem Prep Course

Liebe Schülerinnen, liebe Schüler,

der Prep Course möchte euch in der Vorbereitung auf die Kursstufe unterstützen.
In 5 Units bearbeitet ihr die zentralen Themen des Bildungsplans. In den Units werden insgesamt 18 Skills in Schwerpunkten trainiert, mit denen ihr die zentralen Kompetenzen und Fertigkeiten erwerbt, die man für die schriftlichen und mündlichen Prüfungen in der Kursstufe benötigt.

LISTENING SKILLS	Hörverstehen
READING SKILLS	Leseverstehen
VIEWING SKILLS	Hör-/Sehverstehen
ANALYSIS SKILLS	Text- und Medienkompetenz
MEDIATION SKILLS	Sprachmittlung
COMMUNICATION SKILLS	an Gesprächen teilnehmen
SPEAKING SKILLS	zusammenhängendes Sprechen
WRITING SKILLS	Schreiben

Ein **Farbleitsystem** am oberen Rand der Seiten dient der schnellen Orientierung und verweist auf die **zentralen Skills**, die schwerpunktmäßig in der Unit geübt werden.

Jede Unit beginnt mit einer **Einstiegsdoppelseite**, die in das Thema einführt und durch *Start-up Activities* erste Anregungen zum Nachdenken und Diskutieren gibt.

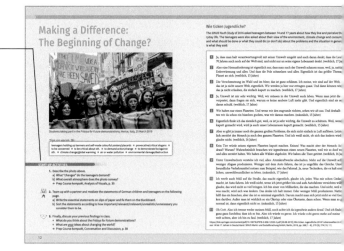

Info-Boxen liefern Zusatz- und Hintergrundinformationen, die bei der Bearbeitung der Aufgaben hilfreich sind.

Jedes Material beginnt mit einer *Awareness-Aufgabe*, die dich auf die Arbeit mit dem Text, Cartoon etc. vorbereitet.

Der **Skill, der im Fokus des Materials steht**, ist mit einem **farbigen Balken** gekennzeichnet. Hier findest du die zentrale Aufgabenstellung.

Die **Webcode-Symbole** zeigen an, dass es zusätzliche Worksheets gibt, die du über www.westermann.de/webcodes downloaden kannst.

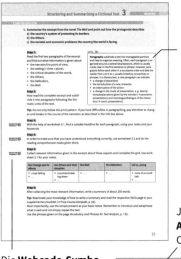

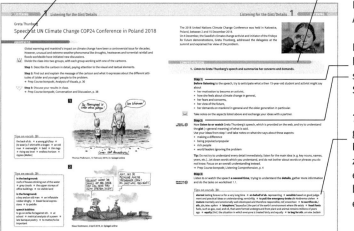

Farbig unterlegte *Steps* helfen dir, die Aufgabenstellung in kleinen Schritten zu bearbeiten.

Tips on vocab-Kästen geben dir Vokabel- und Formulierungshilfen, z. B. für die Beschreibung eines Cartoons oder zum besseren Verständnis eines Hörtextes.

Jedes Material und jede Materialkombination ist mit einem **vollständigen Aufgabenapparat** versehen, der die Anforderungsbereiche *Comprehension, Analysis, Activities* abbildet sowie Aufgaben zu *Grammar/Language* anbietet. Zur **Selbstkontrolle** sind alle Lösungen zu *Grammar/Language*-Aufgaben unter dem Webcode SNG-40217-019 hinterlegt.

Unter den Aufgabenapparaten gibt es **Hinweise** auf den **Prep Course kompakt**, der hinten in das Buch eingelegt ist. Weitere Hilfen gibt es im Anhang (**Appendix**).

Längere Texte sind in **Sinnabschnitte** unterteilt, um dich beim Lesen und Verstehen zu unterstützen.

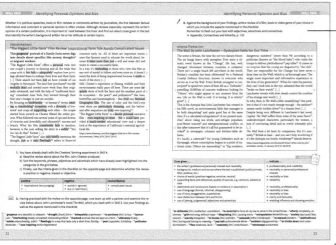

Jede Unit wird mit einer **projektartigen *Skill Task*** (= Lernaufgabe) abgerundet, mit der du in der Unit inhaltlich und methodisch erworbenes Wissen und erlernte Kompetenzen anwenden und erproben kannst.

Vielfältige *Worksheets*, die über **Webcodes** downloadbar sind, unterstützen dich bei der Bearbeitung der unterschiedlichen Aufgabenformate.

Der **Prep Course *kompakt*** stellt eine Vielzahl von *Skills*-Seiten zur Verfügung, die dir kleinschrittig erklären und Beispiele geben, wie du ein Material bearbeiten kannst und worauf du besonders achten solltest.

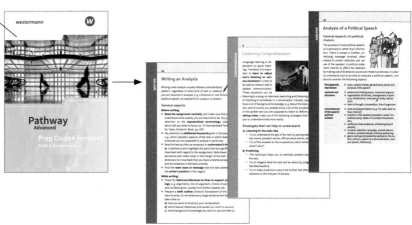

Viel Erfolg und viel Freude bei der Arbeit mit dem Prep Course wünscht euch das Pathway Advanced-Team.

Standardized Terminology for Tasks (*Operatoren*)

In order to enable you to better understand and deal with the tasks in this coursebook, the following list gives you a survey of the key words and standardized formulations for tasks (*Operatoren*) used in the German *Zentralabitur*. Each key word is connected with a definition that not only explains the term itself but also shows you what you are expected to do in order to fulfil this task.

Key word/ terminology	Example	Definition	What you are expected to do
Level I: Orientation/comprehension/understanding/reproduction of texts			
define *bestimmen/ umreißen/ definieren*	Define the meaning of the term multi-cultural.	give a clear, precise meaning/explanation of a term/idea	• before writing, highlight/underline specific details in the text • you should refer to details but do not write wordy explanations – be as precise and specific as possible • make references to lines in the text but do not quote – paraphrase instead
describe *beschreiben*	Describe the woman's appearance.	give/present an accurate/a detailed account of sth./sb.	
state *angeben/sagen/ Gründe angeben*	State briefly the main development of the ecology movement.	specify clearly	
outline *darstellen*	Outline the author's stance on immigration.	work out the main features, structure or general principles of a topic – but omit minor details	• focus on the structure of the text, e. g. how the author develops his/her line of argument or how a story develops, etc. • divide the text into paragraphs • make references to lines/arguments etc. in the text but do not quote – paraphrase instead
present *darstellen*	Present the situation of Asians in London.	(re-)structure and write down	
point out *beschreiben/ erläutern*	Point out the author's main ideas on …	find and explain certain aspects	• focus on the most relevant aspects/ideas/ arguments of the text and avoid details • make references to lines/aspects in the text but do not quote – paraphrase instead
sum up, summarize, write a summary *zusammenfassen*	Summarize the information given in the text about the American Dream.	give a concise account of the main points	• before writing a summary, underline the most relevant aspects in the text – avoid details • use your own words to paraphrase main aspects: do not quote from the text/do not use direct speech (!); do not refer to certain lines etc. in the text • be factual and precise → Prep Course *kompakt*, Writing a Summary, p. 62

Key word/ terminology	Example	Definition	What you are expected to do
Level II: Analysis and re-structuring of texts			
analyse/examine *analysieren/ untersuchen*	Analyse the opposing views on immigration presented in the text. Examine the author's use of language.	describe and explain in detail certain aspects and/ or features of a text	• focus on the structure of the text and pay attention to details • formulate a connecting sentence (contents → analysis) at the beginning • be as precise as possible by using the correct terms and expressions • use quotations/direct references to lines in the text to prove the accuracy of your analysis → Prep Course *kompakt*, Analysis of a Fictional Text, p. 18 → Prep Course *kompakt*, Analysis of a Non-Fictional Text, p. 22 → Appendix, Vocabulary and Phrases for Text Analysis, p. 133 → Appendix, Connectives and Adverbs, p. 120
characterize/write a characterization *charakterisieren/im Detail beschreiben und erklären*	Characterize/Write a characterization of the main character in the play.	analyse the typical features of sb., then describe, explain and interpret the way in which the character(s) is/are presented	• highlight/underline important details about the character and take notes in the margin, using different colours for specific devices • pay attention to details: do not cover everything but focus on the most striking devices/details • use quotations/direct references to lines in the text to prove the accuracy of your analysis → Prep Course *kompakt*, Characterization of a Figure in Literature, p. 34
explain *erklären*	Explain the protagonist's obsession with money.	describe and define in detail	• highlight/underline important details in the text and take notes in the margin, using different colours for specific devices • pay attention to details: do not cover everything but focus on the most striking devices/details • refer directly to certain lines/arguments etc. and use quotations and/or refer to lines in the text • be as precise as possible by using the correct terms and expressions → Prep Course *kompakt*, Analysis of a Fictional Text, p. 18 and Analysis of a Non-Fictional Text, p. 22
interpret *interpretieren*	Interpret the message the author wishes to convey.	make clear the meaning of sth.	• try to read "between the lines" and use your background knowledge • do not give wordy explanations and opinions but be as specific and precise as possible • refer directly to certain lines/arguments etc. and use quotations and/or refer to lines in the text
compare *vergleichen*	Compare the view of the two writers on recycling. Compare the behaviour of the women.	point out similarities and/or differences of things/characters/ situations	• before writing your comparison, underline the most relevant differences/similarities in the text using different colours • make a table in two columns and compare/ juxtapose the different aspects and details • refer directly to certain lines/arguments etc. and use quotations and/or refer to lines in the text

Key word/ terminology	Example	Definition	What you are expected to do
Level III: Discussion/evaluation/text production			
comment (on) *Stellung nehmen*	Comment on the statement that the American Dream is over.	state clearly your opinions/views on a topic and support your views with evidence/arguments/reference to the text(s)	• before writing your text, make a table in two columns and juxtapose views/arguments/ evidence that refer to the argument <u>and</u> the counterargument of the matter • give your opinion on the topic/matter but do not be personal – your judgment should be based on evidence and facts
evaluate *einschätzen/ einordnen/ bewerten*	Evaluate the author's view on the impact of global migration.	form an opinion after carefully considering a topic/question and presenting advantages and disadvantages	• connect aspects/arguments given in the text with your background knowledge and further references • be careful not to just reproduce something that you have learned by heart but paraphrase and refer to the most specific/exemplary aspects • finish your text with a concluding sentence → Prep Course *kompakt*, Basic Types of Non-Fictional Texts, p. 8 → Prep Course *kompakt*, Conversation and Discussion, p. 38
assess *beurteilen*	Assess the importance of standards in education.	make a judgement after thinking carefully about the points for and against sth.	
discuss * *erörtern*	Discuss the consequences of consumerism as referred to in the text.	investigate or examine by argument; give reasons/examples for and against	• weigh different arguments and counter-arguments of a matter • try to take different positions on an issue • collect ideas/arguments and structure them before writing your text • finish your text with a conclusion that summarizes the most important aspects • do not express your own opinion but refer to aspects dealt with in the text → Prep Course *kompakt*, Conversation and Discussion, p. 38
justify *rechtfertigen/ begründen*	You are a CEO of a company. Justify your decision to give a microcredit loan to a village in Nigeria.	show adequate grounds for decisions and conclusions	• before writing your text, collect reasons and examples that support your decision • consider the weight of your arguments/reasons and structure them • finish your text with a concluding and summarizing statement → Prep Course *kompakt*, Conversation and Discussion, p.38
contrast *gegenüberstellen*	Contrast the main characters' opposing views on the USA.	emphasize the difference between two or more things	• before writing your text, make a table in two columns and juxtapose views/arguments/ evidence that refer to the argument <u>and</u> the counterargument of the matter • refer directly to certain lines/arguments etc. and use quotations and/or refer to lines in the text • collect ideas/arguments and structure them before writing your text

* The task "Discuss (in class)" focuses on an oral activity together with a group rather than a written evaluation of a topic.

Key word/ terminology	Example	Definition	What you are expected to do
prove *am Text belegen*	Prove the effects of Western values on developing countries.	give evidence to provide a clear and convincing argument	• before writing your text, collect ideas about the respective matter and structure them • give examples and refer to background information on relevant aspects/arguments • do not give wordy explanations and opinions; be as specific and precise as possible • refer directly to certain lines/arguments etc. and use quotations and/or refer to lines in the text → Prep Course *kompakt*, Basic Types of Non-Fictional Texts, p. 8
reflect on *reflektieren/ bedenken*	Reflect on how the author deals with the problem of exploiting workers in sweatshops.	express your thoughts in a carefully considered and balanced way	• before writing, underline/highlight key words and relevant aspects in the text • collect ideas on how you want to respond to the matter • weigh different aspects/arguments by juxtaposing them in a table • you may state your opinion on the issue but avoid being personal – be factual and precise • finish your text with a concluding and summarizing statement → Prep Course *kompakt*, Conversation and Discussion, p. 38

Task Marker

START-UP ACTIVITIES	Reactivating knowledge, preparing the new topic, introducing the new unit
AWARENESS	Introducing a new text or material, giving an impetus
COMPREHENSION	Tasks for the understanding, comprehension nd reproduction of texts/material
ANALYSIS	Tasks for the analysis, examination and interpretation of texts/material
ACTIVITIES	Tasks for further discussion, creative writing, discussion, presentation, etc.
GRAMMAR/LANGUAGE	Reactivating grammar and language skills, grammar exercises in context.

Symbols

 Group work, work in a team, work with a partner

 Communication training, e.g. discussion, debate, role play, etc.

M Mediation between English and German

/ Creative writing task

 Presentation of projects, results of group work or research

@ Internet research

metaphor* This * sign indicates that the word/term can be found in the Literary Terms section (pp. 135 ff.).

SNG-40217-001 Worksheet 1.1 @ Webcodes refer to additional material, e.g. worksheets, weblinks to audio or audiovisual material. Visit the following website www.westermann.de/webcode and enter the respective code.

Making a Difference:
The Beginning of Change?

Students taking part in the *Fridays for Future* demonstrations; Venice, Italy, 25 March 2019

Tips on vocab »

teenagers holding up banners and self-made colourful posters/placards ▪ provocative/critical slogans ▪ to be concerned ▪ to be critical about sth. ▪ to demand action/change ▪ to demonstrate for/against sth. ▪ climate change/global warming ▪ air or water pollution ▪ environmental damage/destruction

START-UP ACTIVITIES

1. Describe the photo above.
   a) What "changes" do the teenagers demand?
   b) What overall atmosphere does the photo convey?
   → Prep Course *kompakt*, Analysis of Visuals, p. 30

2. Team up with a partner and mediate the statements of German children and teenagers on the following page.
   a) Write the essential statements on slips of paper and fix them on the blackboard.
   b) Sort the statements according to how important/relevant/irrelevant/unrealistic/unnecessary you consider them to be.

3. Finally, discuss your previous findings in class.
   ● What do you think about the *Fridays for Future* demonstrations?
   ● What are your ideas about changing the world?
   → Prep Course *kompakt*, Conversation and Discussion, p. 38

Wie ticken Jugendliche?

The *SINUS Youth Study* of 2016 asked teenagers between 14 and 17 years about how they live and perceive their everyday life. The teenagers were also asked about their view of the environment, climate change and consumption – and what should be done or what they could do (or don't do) about the problems and the situation in general. Here is what they said:

1. Ja, dass man halt verantwortungsvoll mit seiner Umwelt umgeht und auch daran denkt, dass die Leute in 70 Jahren auch noch auf der Welt sind, und nicht nur an seine eigene Lebenszeit denkt. (weiblich, 17 Jahre)

2. Also eine Herausforderung ist eigentlich nur, dass man nach der Umwelt schauen muss, weil, ja, natürlich Erderwärmung und alles. Und dass die Pole schmelzen und alles. Eigentlich ist das größte Thema der Planet an sich. (weiblich, 15 Jahre)

3. Die Verschmutzung im Wald und im Meer, das ist ganz schlimm. Ich meine, wir sind auf der Welt, aber das ist ja nicht unsere Welt, eigentlich. Wir werden ja hier nur ertragen quasi. Und dann können wir uns das ja nicht erlauben, die einfach kaputt zu machen. (weiblich, 17 Jahre)

4. Ja, Umwelt ist mir sehr wichtig. Weil, wir müssen in der Umwelt auch leben. Wenn man jetzt die Luft verpestet, dann fragen sie sich, warum es keine saubere Luft mehr gibt. Und eigentlich sind sie selber daran schuld. (weiblich, 17 Jahre)

5. Wir haben nur einen Planeten. Und wenn wir den zugrunde richten, sehen wir alt aus. Und deshalb sollten wir da schon ein bisschen gucken, was wir daraus machen. (männlich, 15 Jahre)

6. Eigentlich finde ich das ziemlich gut, weil, es ist ja sehr wichtig, die Umwelt zu schützen. Weil, wenn die kaputt gemacht wird, wird ja auch unser Lebensraum kaputt gemacht. (weiblich, 15 Jahre)

7. Aber es gibt ja immer noch die ganzen großen Probleme, die sich nicht einfach in Luft auflösen. Letztendlich zerstört der Mensch ja auch den ganzen Planeten. Und ich weiß nicht, ob sich das ändern wird. Ich glaube nicht. (weiblich, 16 Jahre)

8. Kein Tier würde seinen eigenen Planeten kaputt machen. Keines! Was macht aber der Mensch: Scheiß drauf! Warum? Wahrscheinlich brauchen wir irgendwann einen neuen Planeten, weil wir so doof waren und alles zerstört haben. Wir haben alle Wälder abgeholzt. Wir haben alle Tiere getötet. (weiblich, 16 Jahre)

9. Unter Umweltschutz verstehe ich viel, alles: Atomkraftwerke abschalten. Mehr auf die Umwelt achten, weniger Abgase produzieren. Weniger mit dem Auto fahren, das ist ja ungefähr das Gleiche. Umweltfreundliche Verkehrsmittel nutzen zum Beispiel, wie das Fahrrad. Ja, neue Techniken, die es halt ermöglichen, umweltfreundlicher zu leben. (männlich, 17 Jahre)

10. Ich werfe auch Müll auf die Straße, das macht eigentlich, glaube ich, jeder. Was mir schon Gedanken macht, ist Auto fahren. Ich weiß nicht, wenn ich jetzt größer bin und aufs Autofahren verzichten will, ich glaube, das wird nicht so viel bringen. Ich bin einer von Milliarden, die das machen. Und nicht, weil einer was macht, wird sich was ändern. Das denke ich halt immer. Oder weniger Müll produzieren. Natürlich hilft das ein bisschen, aber das ist so minimal eigentlich. Darum macht man sich jetzt nicht so viel Gedanken darüber. Außer man ist wirklich so ein Ökotyp oder eine Ökotante, dann schon. Wenn man so ganz normal ist, dann eigentlich nicht so. (männlich, 15 Jahre)

11. Oh Gott. Also ich trenne weder meinen Müll, noch achte ich da irgendwie anders drauf. Und ich finde das ganz ganz furchtbar, dass ich so bin. Also ich würde es gerne. Ich würde echt gerne mehr auf meine Umwelt achten, aber ich bin zu faul. (weiblich, 17 Jahre)

https://link.springer.com/content/pdf/10.1007%2F978-3-658-12533-2.pdf [20.08.2019]; Wie ticken Jugendliche 2016? Lebenswelten im Alter von 14 bis 17 Jahren in Deutschland. SINUS Markt- und Sozialforschung GmbH, Berlin, 2016, pp. 268 (1 – 8), 270 (9), 274 (10, 11)

Greta Thunberg
Speech at UN Climate Change COP24 Conference in Poland 2018

AWARENESS

Global warming and mankind's impact on climate change have been a controversial issue for decades. However, unusual and extreme weather phenomena like droughts, heatwaves and torrential rainfall and floods worldwide have initiated new discussions.

 Divide the class into two groups, with each group working with one of the cartoons.

Step 1: Describe the cartoon in detail, paying attention to the visual and textual elements.

Step 2: Find out and explain the message of the cartoon and what it expresses about the different attitudes of (older and younger) people to the problem.
→ Prep Course *kompakt*, Analysis of Visuals, p. 30

 Step 3: Discuss your results in class.
→ Prep Course *kompakt*, Conversation and Discussion, p. 38

Tips on vocab »»»

the back of sb. ■ a young girl/boy ■ (to wear) a T-shirt with a slogan ■ an old man ■ overweight ■ bald ■ thin legs ■ rising sea level ■ endless horizon ■ ripples (*Wellen*)

Thomas Plaßmann, 12 February 2019, in: Spiegel online

Tips on vocab »»»

in the background:
roofs of houses sticking out of the water ■ grey clouds ■ the upper storeys of office buildings ■ no visible land

in the foreground:
a boy and an old man ■ an inflatable rubber dinghy ■ bleak facial expressions ■ to paddle

speech bubbles:
to go on strike for/against sth. ■ at school ■ metrical analysis of a poem ■ late baroque poetry ■ to matter/to be important

Klaus Stuttmann, 2 April 2019, in: Spiegel online

The 2018 United Nations Climate Change Conference was held in Katowice, Poland, between 2 and 15 December 2018.

On 4 December, the Swedish climate change activist and initiator of the *Fridays for Future* demonstrations, Greta Thunberg, addressed the delegates at the summit and explained her view of the problem.

COMPREHENSION

1. Listen to Greta Thunberg's speech and summarize her concerns and demands.

Step 1:
Before listening to the speech, try to anticipate what a then 15-year-old student and activist might say about

- her motivation to become an activist,
- how she feels about climate change in general,
- her fears and concerns,
- her view of the future,
- her demands on mankind in general and the older generation in particular.

 Take notes on the aspects listed above and exchange your ideas with a partner.

Step 2:

Webcode
SNG-40217-001

Now **listen to or watch** Greta Thunberg's speech, which is provided on the web, and try to understand the **gist** (= general meaning) of what is said.

Use your ideas from step 1 and take notes on what she says about these aspects:

- making a difference
- being popular/unpopular
- rich people
- world leaders ignoring the problem

Tip: Do not try to understand every detail immediately; listen for the main idea (e. g. key nouns, names, years, etc.). Jot down words which you understand, and do not bother about words or phrases you do not know. Focus on an overall understanding instead.

→ Prep Course *kompakt*, Listening Comprehension, p. 4

Step 3:

SNG-40217-001
Worksheet 1.1

Listen to or watch the speech **a second time**, trying to understand the **details**, gather more information and do the tasks on worksheet 1.1.

Tips on vocab »»

eternal lasting forever or for a very long time ■ **on behalf of sb.** representing ■ **sensible** based on good judgement and practical ideas or understanding; *vernünftig* ■ **to pull the emergency brake** *die Notbremse ziehen* ■ **mature** mentally and emotionally well-developed and therefore responsible; *reif, erwachsen* ■ **to sacrifice sb./ sth.** *jdn./etw. opfern* ■ **biosphere** [ˈbaɪəʊsfɪər] the part of the earth's environment where life exists ■ **fossil fuels** fuels, such as gas, coal, and oil, that were formed underground from plant and animal remains millions of years ago ■ **equity** (*fml.*) the situation in which everyone is treated fairly and equally ■ **to beg for sth.** *um etw. betteln*

Step 4:

Now, write a summary of the speech in about 150 – 200 words, using your notes. Try to use your own words and follow **the introduction – main part – conclusion pattern**. First, write an introductory sentence that answers the w-questions.

Be careful to use the simple present and do not use any direct speech or quotations.

→ Prep Course *kompakt*, Writing a Summary, p. 62

Begin like this: *In a speech, given to the 2018 Climate Change Conference in Katowice, Poland, the 15-year-old Swedish climate change activist Greta Thunberg, expresses her concerns about …*

Tips on vocab >>>>>

> to deliver a speech ■ to address an audience/representatives from … ■ to be critical about ■ to express concerns ■ to demand action ■ to accuse sb. of sth. ■ to blame sb. for sth. ■ in the name of profit ■ to be hypocritical/a hypocrite (*scheinheilig/ein(e) Scheinheilige(r) sein*) ■ to threaten sb. ■ to underestimate sb.'s ability or power

ANALYSIS >>>>>>

2. First, divide the class into four groups, with each group working on one of the topics below. Then, examine Greta Thunberg's abilities as a speaker and her use of rhetorical devices*.

Focus particularly on her use of
- personal pronouns (e. g. I – you – us – we – our),
- conditional clauses/if-clauses,
- repetition (anaphora*, parallelism*),
- sentence structure.

Remember to explain the function and effect of these devices.

→ Prep Course *kompakt*, Analysis of a Political Speech, p. 26

3. Although Greta Thunberg's initiative has gained enormous publicity and many supporters, there are critical voices about *Fridays on Future* as well.

An American pen pal of yours has asked you about the *Fridays for Future* initiative and how people and the media react to it in Germany.

M   Mediate the critical comment *Geht zur Schule* by Nils Minkmar, which was published in the German weekly magazine *Der Spiegel*.

Explain to your friend what Minkmar thinks about
- the importance of civilization, human rights and culture,
- the importance of and need for compulsory schooling,
- the privilege of attending school,
- the importance of striking against mass consumption.

→ Prep Course *kompakt*, Mediation, p. 36

ACTIVITIES >>>>>>

4. Comment critically on and evaluate Greta Thunberg's speech.

What aspects of her statements might be appealing or threatening to the listeners?

→ Prep Course *kompakt*, Writing a Comment and a Review, p. 52

5. Find further information about Greta Thunberg and her climate activism.
Prepare short presentations about your findings in class.

→ Prep Course *kompakt*, Presentations, p. 44

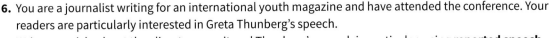

GRAMMAR / LANGUAGE ►►►►►►►

6. You are a journalist writing for an international youth magazine and have attended the conference. Your readers are particularly interested in Greta Thunberg's speech.
Write an article about the climate summit and Thunberg's speech in particular, using **reported speech** and **paraphrasing** (cf. Skill 9, p. 60) to report the essential parts of the speech.
Remember to backshift tenses where necessary and to formulate an introductory sentence.

Examples:
- Greta explained that she spoke on behalf of Climate Justice Now.
- She added that she had learned that you are never …

→ Appendix, Indirect Speech, p. 122
→ Appendix, Tenses, p. 130

Nils Minkmar

Geht zur Schule

In der Diskussion um den Schutz[1] des Klimas hört man oft, es gehe darum, die Erde zu retten. Die aber wird auch noch stark erwärmt, überflutet oder tiefgefroren ihre Bahnen ziehen[2]. So wie die anderen Planeten auch. ₅ Was vor dem Folgen des Klimawandels gerettet werden soll, ist die menschliche Zivilisation, Städte, Landwirtschaft[3], Menschenrechte, Kultur – das ganze Programm dessen, was unser Leben lebenswert[4] macht.

Und hier stoßen wir auf das Problem, das ich mit der ₁₀ freitäglichen Schulstreikbewegung habe. Das Anliegen[5] teile ich, in Wahrheit sind wir alle noch viel zu ruhig angesichts der ökologischen Gefahr. Aber das Mittel, den Schulstreik am Freitag, lehne ich ab. Auch wenn es nur wenige Stunden sind, es berührt ein Prinzip. Die Schul-₁₅ pflicht[6] ist eine der bedeutendsten Errungenschaften[7] der Menschheit. Sie schützt Kinder vor Ignoranz und Ausbeutung[8], vor elterlicher und politischer Willkür[9]. Die Schulpflicht verhindert Kinderarbeit und ermöglicht erst die Autonomie des Denkens und des Handelns.

₂₀ Ich habe öfter von Menschen, die schon lange leben, gehört, wie sehr sie es bedauern[10], in einer von Krieg und Not gezeichneten Jugend nicht die Möglichkeit gehabt zu haben, länger die Schule zu besuchen. Auch wenn sie später einen Beruf fanden – die Trauer[11] um Lernzeit, die nur dem Kind gehörte, das sie einmal waren, bleibt. ₂₅ Es gehört zur Schülerfolklore[12], auf die Schule zu schimpfen[13] – aber das darf nicht darüber hinwegtäuschen[14], dass der Schulbesuch ein schwer erkämpftes Privileg der Kinder und Jugendlichen ist. Bildung befreit und ermöglicht stets noch mehr davon – aber wer ₃₀ an dieser Stelle streikt, blockiert seine Möglichkeiten. Er verringert[15] seine Macht.

Wie die Schulpflicht ist auch das Streikrecht[16] eine späte, schöne Errungenschaft. Ein guter Streik tut ziemlich weh, ein Schulstreik aber, der sich nicht auf eine Verbes-₃₅ serung der Schule bezieht, ist für den Rest der klimazerstörenden[17] Gesellschaft kein Problem. Anders sieht es mit einem Konsumstreik gegen ressourcenverschlingende[18] Billigtextilien oder Fast-Food-Ketten aus. Jugendliche, die nichts mehr kaufen, sind das wahre spät-₄₀ kapitalistische[19] Schreckgespenst[20].

Nils Minkmar, DER SPIEGEL 13/2019, 22.03.2019, p. 109

[1] protection of – [2] to follow its path – [3] agriculture – [4] liveable – [5] concerns, objectives – [6] compulsory education – [7] achievement – [8] exploitation – [9] arbitrariness – [10] to regret sth. – [11] grief, sorrow – [12] student habits – [13] to rant about sth. – [14] to hide the fact that … – [15] to diminish – [16] right to strike – [17] climate-wrecking – [18] … that deplete natural resources – [19] late capitalist – [20] horror, nightmare

Tracy Geoghegan

Global Childhood Report 2019: Changing Lives in Our Lifetime

AWARENESS

The cover page of the 2019 *Global Childhood Report* shows 11-year-old Djeneba, a sixth-grade student from Mali, who appears to be a happy and healthy child. However, there are many more factors that determine childhood.

SNG-40217-002
Worksheet 2.1

a) Team up with a partner and work with the various information given on worksheet 2.1.

b) Discuss in class: What do you consider to be the most/least relevant factors that determine a happy and healthy childhood? Make a ranking of these factors.

What has changed in 100 years?

Millions of children are alive and thriving today because of medical and technological advances[1] we tend to take for granted. Breakthrough discoveries of vaccines[2] to
5 prevent childhood diseases, coupled with better care for mothers and babies, have saved countless lives and improved overall health. The world has also made good progress in building human and institutional capacity to deliver lifesaving solutions to the hardest to reach
10 and most vulnerable[3] children.

But perhaps the most important change in the last 100 years is how we think about children. In 1919, when Eglantyne Jebb founded *Save the Children*, her conviction that children have a right to food, health care and
15 education and protection from exploitation was not a mainstream idea. The *Declaration on the Rights of the Child*, drafted[4] by Jebb, was adopted by the League of Nations[5] in 1924. It asserted[6] these rights for all children and made it the duty of the international community to
20 put children's rights in the forefront of planning. *The Convention on the Rights of the Child*, which was adopted in 1989 and has been ratified by all but one country, further changed the way children are viewed and treated – as human beings with a distinct[7] set of rights, in-
25 stead of as passive objects of care and charity.

As these visionary frameworks[8] have gained acceptance, public opinion about children has been slowly but steadily shifting worldwide. For example, more people around the world now believe children belong in school,
30 not toiling[9] in fields and factories. And more governments have enacted[10] laws to prevent child labour and child marriage, and make school free and mandatory[11]

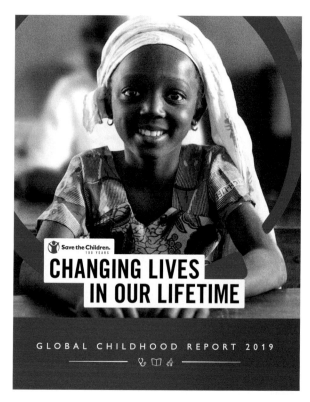

for all children, regardless of their gender, race, refugee status or special needs.

The world has come a long way in 100 years, but we still 35
have a long way to go to ensure every child, everywhere grows up healthy, educated and protected from harm.

Fewer children are forced into work

Much of the decline in child labour in recent years has been credited to active policy efforts to extend and im- 40

[1] **advance** the forward moving or improvement of sth. – [2] **vaccine** *Impfstoff* – [3] **vulnerable** *verletzlich* – [4] **to draft sth.** to write a document for the first time, including the main points; *etw. entwerfen* – [5] **League of Nations** *Völkerbund*; an intergovernmental organization founded in 1920 as a result of the Paris Peace Conference that ended the First World War – [6] **to assert** (*fml.*) to say that sth. is certainly true – [7] **distinct** clearly noticeable – [8] **framework** a system of rules, ideas or beliefs that is used to plan or decide sth. – [9] **to toil** to work very hard – [10] **to enact** to make sth. law – [11] **mandatory** *verpflichtend*

prove schooling, extend social protection, expand basic services, and establish legal frameworks against child labour.

Globally, there has been better progress in reducing child labour among older children than among younger ones. The number of child labourers aged 12 to 17 has fallen 42 per cent, from 136 million in 2000 to 79 million today. During the same period, child labour among 5- to 11-year-olds fell by a third, from 110 million in 2000 to 73 million today. These young child labourers are of particular concern, as they are most vulnerable to workplace abuses and compromised education.

The most dramatic gains in ending child labour have been in eastern Europe and Central Asia. Uzbekistan cut[12] its child labour rate by an impressive 92 per cent [...]. Albania's child labour rate is down by as much as 79 per cent [...]. Azerbaijan, Belarus, Moldova and Ukraine each appear to have reduced their child labour rate among 5- to 14-year-olds by more than 60 per cent. Economic growth, poverty reduction and political commitments[13] have led to significant progress in this region. Each of the countries above has ratified[14] the International Labour Organization (ILO) child labour conventions. But while countries in this region have made progress in reducing child labour among 5- to 14-year-olds, almost all other child labourers in the region today are involved in hazardous[15] work.

> ## HUNDREDS OF MILLIONS OF CHILDREN HAVE BEEN SAVED
>
> Global progress has saved millions of childhoods since the year 2000. Now there are:
>
> - 4.4 million fewer child deaths per year
> - 49 million fewer stunted[19] children
> - 115 million fewer children out of chool
> - 94 million fewer child laborers
> - 11 million fewer teen births per year
> - 12,000 fewer child homicides[20] per year

Mexico has made impressive progress against child labour, cutting its rate by 80 per cent [...].

Vietnam's successful work to reduce poverty has improved living conditions for many families and reduced the need to send children to work. The country has invested heavily in education, ensuring high enrolment[16] rates, with a particular emphasis on ethnic minority children in remote mountainous areas. Mass media and international NGOs have helped to raise awareness of child rights and the harmful effects of child labour. Currently, Vietnam is implementing a national programme to prevent and minimize child labour from 2016 to 2020. [...]

Despite global progress, there are still 152 million children engaged in child labour – nearly 1 in 10 children worldwide – with almost half of them (73 million) in hazardous work that directly endangers their health, safety and emotional development. A hypothetical country made up only of these child labourers would rank as the world's ninth largest. Unless progress is accelerated[17], 121 million children will be engaged in child labour in 2025. Nearly half of the world's child labourers live in Africa (72 million). [...]

In contrast to all other regions, child labour has actually increased in sub-Saharan Africa. A breakthrough in this region will be critical[18] to ending child labour worldwide.

https://resourcecentre.savethechildren.net/node/15264/pdf/global_childhood_report_2019_english.pdf, pp. 3, 23 f. [20.08.2019]

COMPREHENSION ⫸⫸⫸⫸

1. **Outline the excerpt from the *Global Childhood Report* and state which developments and improvements it highlights.**

Step 1:
In order to get a general overview and understanding of the text,
a) read the text first.
b) Then, do the comprehension task on worksheet 2.2.

SNG-40217-002 @
Worksheet 2.2

---

[12] **to cut sth.** to make sth. smaller; to reduce sth. – [13] **commitment** *Verpflichtungserklärung* – [14] **to ratify sth.** (*fml.*) to make an agreement official – [15] **hazardous** ['hæzərdəs] dangerous and likely to cause damage – [16] **enrolment** *Einschreibung (offizielle Anmeldung)* – [17] **to accelerate** to increase the speed of sth. – [18] **critical** here: of the greatest importance to make sth. law – [19] **stunted** prevented from growing or developing to the usual size; *körperlich zurückgeblieben* – [20] **homicide** (an) act of murder

Step 2:

In a second, **close reading**, identify relevant keywords and key phrases that help you to get a deeper understanding of the text and its details.

The Info box below gives you some help in what to look for.

Info 〉〉〉〉

Generally, **keywords** and **key phrases** are important when identifying the content and message of a text, and necessary for analysis of the text later on.

Keywords and **key phrases**

- are significant words which support details and messages of the text.
- are often repeated several times throughout the text.
- represent the main ideas of the author.
- can often be found in the headline/title of a text or at the beginning or conclusion of a paragraph.
- identify the topic of the text.
- are often descriptive (*beschreibend*) and/or illustrative (*veranschaulichend*).
- often occur in word fields or word groups.

Step 3:

After identifying and extracting the relevant keywords, it can be helpful to sort them in graphic organizers (e. g. a timeline, a flow chart, a mind map, etc.).

Tip: Include the statistical data given on p. 19.

Example:

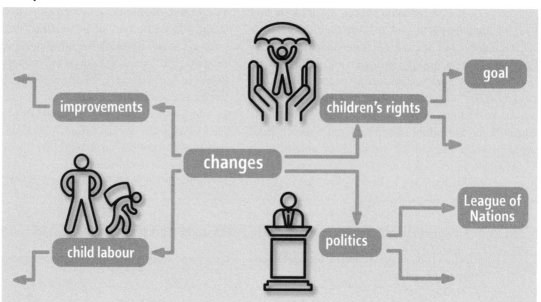

Step 4:

The text itself and the added statistics contain a lot of data and figures, some of which are rather general, others very precise.

Use the grid provided on worksheet 2.3 to sort and organize the statistical information.

Step 5:

Display your grids in class and discuss the developments and changes since 1919.

Step 6:

Using your results and findings, write an outline of the text.

Tip: Pay attention to the term 'outline' and keep in mind that it requires you to
- focus on the structure of the text,
- work out the main aspects, but leave out the more minor details.

→ Standardized Terminology for Tasks, p. 8

ANALYSIS ⫸

2. The excerpt is taken from is a report highlighting the 100th anniversary of the work of the NGO *Save the Children*. As can be expected, the report wants to acknowledge the NGO's work and praise the positive developments and changes their work has achieved.
   Give examples from the text that highlight the NGO's work and explain their function in detail.
   → Prep Course *kompakt*, Analysis of a Non-Fictional Text, p. 22

3. Examine and analyse the stylistic devices that have been employed to highlight the NGO's work and success.
   → Prep Course *kompakt*, Analysis of a Non-Fictional Text, p. 22

ACTIVITIES ⫸

4. As the report points out, there have been fundamental changes in the life of children worldwide in the past decades.
   Do a project in class on the topic and interview your older relatives (parents, grandparents, etc.) about
   a) what their childhood was like,
   b) what they hoped for and dreamed of,
   c) what changes concerning children's rights, etc. they have experienced in their lives.

@ 5. Do research on Eglantyne Jebb (1876 – 1926), the founder of *Save the Children*.
   Prepare 5-minute presentations and share your findings in class.
   → Prep Course *kompakt*, Presentations, p. 44

GRAMMAR / LANGUAGE ⫸

6. Despite all the achievements that have already been made, *Save the Children* is planning ahead and setting new goals for the future.
   You are a speaker of *Save the Children* and are introducing the NGO's plans to the public. Use different **future tenses** (future I, future II, going-to future, will future) to express your plans and future activities.

   Examples:
   - By 2030, we **will have reduced** child labour by a further 30 %. (future II)
   - Next year, **we're going to talk** to further government representatives and … (going- to future)

   → Appendix, Tenses, p. 130

John Lanchester

The Wall

Step 1: Worldwide, about 258 million people – so-called migrants – have left their native country because they want to start a better life somewhere else.
In class, collect ideas about the possible causes and people's reasons to migrate.

Tip: The Tips on vocab box on the right will help you to formulate your first ideas.

Tips on vocab ⟫

to seek refuge ▪ to escape war/poverty/ persecution ▪ to seek a better life ▪ political/religious persecution ▪ torture ▪ to improve your prospects ▪ economic refugee ▪ to participate in sth. ▪ to suffer from ▪ to be denied basic rights ▪ to hope for

Step 2: Over the years, several hundred thousand migrants have tried to reach Europe's shores, crossing the Mediterranean and attempting to enter countries like Spain, Italy, Malta and Greece.
Team up with a partner and describe the cartoon below, paying attention to the visual and textual elements.

Klaus Stuttmann, 13 July 2019, in: Spiegel online

Tips on vocab ⟫

on the right: castle complex ▪ fortress (*Festung*) ▪ massive stone walls with battlements (*Zinnen*) ▪ keep (*Burgfried*) ▪ watchtowers ▪ embrasure (*Schießscharte*) ▪ steep shore with rocks ▪ flag of the European Union ▪ speech bubble

on the left: to capsize (*kentern*) ▪ (rowing) boat ▪ silhouettes of people ▪ (yellow) life vests ▪ to drown

Step 3: First, compare your findings in class. Then, try to explain the message of the cartoon. What attitude and behaviour does the German cartoonist Klaus Stuttmann describe and criticize?

In his 2019 novel, *The Wall*, the British author John Lanchester describes the life of the protagonist, Joseph Kavanagh, who begins his obligatory 2-year turn of duty on the Wall, a security system surrounding the British coastline. The novel is set in a near-future dystopian[1] British society.

1 Sometimes we would be told about a flotilla[2] of Others who had been spotted and attacked from the air, just in case some of them had survived and might still be coming in our direction. Occasionally there would be
5 some big-picture news about crops[3] failing or countries breaking down or coordination between rich countries, or some other emerging[4] detail of the new world we were occupying since the Change. Sometimes there would be news of an attack in which Others had used
10 new or unexpected tactics, or attacked in surprising strength. If Others ever got through, we were told about it. [...]

Although everybody always calls the Wall the Wall, that isn't its official name. Officially it is the National Coast-
15 al Defence Structure. On official documents it's abbreviated[5] to NCDS. [...]

2 Mornings on the Wall, dawn and dusk[6] and night, were times for poetry. Skyconcretewaterwind. Afternoons were for prose[7]. Ten thousand kilometres of
20 Wall. A Defender for every two hundred metres: fifty thousand Defenders on duty at any time. Another fifty thousand on the other shift, so a hundred thousand on duty, day in day out. Plus it's two weeks on, two weeks off. Half of the Defenders aren't on the Wall, they're on
25 leave or on training or waiting for their two weeks' turn of duty[8]. So two hundred thousand active Defenders at any given moment. Add support and ancillary staff[9], officers and administrators, add the Coast Guard and the air force and the navy, people off[10] sick, whatever, and
30 it's more than three hundred thousand people involved in defending the Wall. That's why everybody goes to the Wall, no exceptions. That's the rule.

3 Except for Breeders[11]. It's a paradox. Because the Wall needs so many people, we need people to Breed, so
35 that there are enough people to man[12] the Wall. It's on a fine edge[13] as things currently stand, and there's talk of the tours having to be made longer, two and a half or three years, to make up[14] a shortfall[15]. But people don't

want to Breed, because the world is such a horrible place. So as an incentive to get people to leave the Wall, 40 if you reproduce, you can leave. You Breed to leave the Wall. Some people say that this isn't fair to the children, who are born into a world where they have to do time on the Wall in their turn. Maybe they won't, though. Maybe all the Others will have died off by then and we 45 won't need the Wall. Who knows? And besides, the children can always Breed in their turn, and get off the Wall that way. Prolonging[16] the life of our species too, as a side effect. Breed to Leave, that's the slogan.

I should say that people don't despise[17] or look down on 50 Breeders. They just think they're a bit weird. It's not so much, that's wrong, it's more, why would you? Why don't people want to Breed? It's an idea that caught on after the Change: that we shouldn't want to bring children into the world. We broke the world and have no 55 right to keep populating it. We can't feed and look after all the humans there already are, here and now; the humans who are here and now, most of them, are starving and drowning, dying and desperate; so how dare we make more of them? They aren't drowning[18] and starv- 60 ing[19] here, in this country, but they are almost everywhere else; so how dare we make more humans to come into this world? There are lots of different answers to that. Nobody can predict the future; that's one answer. God tells us to; that's an answer which works for some. 65 Maybe the best answer, though, or maybe I'm just talking about the one that makes the most sense to me, is just, because. Because; the best/worst answer to most human questions. Why are we here? Because.

4 Back to the prose. Most Defenders stand on the Wall 70 because that's where the manpower is needed, but the Wall isn't the only form of border and coastal protection. The Flight scans the sea for Others, locates them, sometimes 'takes them out' then and there. It's funny, only Defenders on the Wall talk about 'killing' Others: 75 we're the ones who do it face to face, and we're the only

---

[1] **dystopian society** a society in which people do not work well with each other and are not happy – [2] **flotilla** a large group of boats or small ships – [3] **crop** *Ernte* – [4] **to emerge** *sich herausstellen* – [5] **to abbreviate** to make a word shorter by using the first letters of each word – [6] **dusk** the time before night when it is not yet dark – [7] **prose** written language in its ordinary form – [8] **one's turn of duty** *an der Reihe sein, Dienst zu tun* – [9] **ancillary staff** additional, supporting personnel – [10] **to be off** to be not at work – [11] **breeder** sb. who breeds (produces) animals; here: sb. who bears children – [12] **to man sth.** to operate sth. – [13] **to be on an edge** to be at a point where sth. unpleasant is likely to happen – [14] **to make up sth.** (*phr. v.*) *etw. ausgleichen* – [15] **shortfall** *Mangel* – [16] **to prolong sth.** to make sth. last longer – [17] **to despise sb./sth.** *jdn./etw. verachten* – [18] **to drown** *ertrinken* – [19] **to starve** to die from hunger

ones who don't use euphemisms[20] for it. The Flight consists of some people in planes and many more people operating drones. Sometimes the Flight marks their lo-
[80] cation for the Guards, full name Coast Guards but everyone calls them the Guards, who use ships of two main kinds, medium-range and short-range. They patrol the coast and the seas and their job is to sink the Others' boats. The Defenders are there for the rest of the Others:
[85] the ones who get through, which is a significant number, because there is a lot of sky and sea to watch, and because ten thousand kilometres of coast is a lot of coast. They come in rowing boats and rubber dinghies[21], on inflatable tubes[22], in groups and in swarms and in cou-
[90] ples, in threes, in singles; the smaller the number, often, the harder to detect. They are clever, they are desperate, they are ruthless[23], they are fighting for their lives, so all of those things had to be true for us as well. We had to be clever and desperate and ruthless and fight for our lives,
[95] only more so, or we would switch places. I didn't want to die fighting on the Wall, but if it came to it, I would rather that than be put to sea. One in, one out: for every Other who got over the Wall, one Defender would be put to sea. A tribunal[24] of our fellow Defenders would con-
[100] vene[25] and decide who was most responsible, and those people, in that order of responsibility, would be put in a boat that same day. If five Others got over the Wall, five of us would be put to sea. It was easy to imagine being those people. Your old comrades pointing guns at you
[105] while you pushed you boat out into the water, the only feeling colder and lonelier and more final than being on the Wall. [...]

[5] None of us could talk to our parents. By 'us' I mean my generation, people born after the Change. You
[110] know that thing where you break up with someone and say, It's not you, it's me? This is the opposite. It's not us, it's them. Everyone knows what the problem is. The diagnosis isn't hard – the diagnosis isn't even controversial. It's guilt, generational guilt. The olds feel they
[115] irretrievably[26] fucked up[27] the world, then allowed us to be born into it. You know what? It's true. That's exactly what they did. They know it, we know it. Everybody knows it.

To make things worse, the olds didn't do time on the Wall, because there was no Wall, because there had [120] been no Change so the Wall wasn't needed. This means that the single most important and formative[28] experience in the lives of my generations – the big thing we all have in common – is something about which they have exactly no clue. The life advice, the knowing-better, the [125] back-in-our-day wisdom which, according to books and films, was a big part of the whole deal between parents and children, just didn't work. Want to put me straight about what I'm doing wrong in my life, Grandad? No thanks. Why don't you travel back in time and unfuck- [130] up the world and then travel back here and maybe then we can talk.

There are admittedly some people my age who are curious about what things were like before, who like to hear about it, who love the stories and the amazing facts. Put [135] it like this: there are some people my age who have a thing about beaches. They watch movies and TV programmes about beaches, they look at pictures of beaches, they ask the olds what it was like to go to a beach, what it felt like to lie on sand all day, and what was it [140] like to build a sandcastle and watch the water come in and see the sandcastle fight off the water and then succumb to[29] it, a castle which once looked so big and invulnerable[30], just melting away, so that when the tide[31] goes out you can't see that there was ever anything [145] there, and what was it like to have a picnic on the beach, didn't sand get in the food, and what was surfing like, what was it like to be carried towards a beach on a wave, with people standing on the beach watching you, and was it really true the water was sometimes warm, even [150] here, even this far north? There are people who love all this shit. Not me. Show me an actual beach, and I'll express some interest in beaches. But you know what? The level of my interest exactly corresponds to the number of existing beaches. And there isn't a single [155] beach left, anywhere in the world.

Not everyone agrees with me on this. Maybe most people don't. Lots of people like to watch old movies where everyone is on the beach all the time. My view? Stupid.

from *The Wall* by John Lanchester. Faber & Faber, London, 2019, pp. 9 ff.

---

[20] **euphemism** [ˈjuːfəmɪzm] *beschönigende Umschreibung* – [21] **dinghy** [ˈdɪŋgi] a small open (sailing) boat – [22] **inflatable tube** *aufblasbare Röhre* – [23] **ruthless** *cruel* – [24] **tribunal** [traɪˈbjuːnl] a special court chosen, esp. by a government, to examine a particular problem – [25] **to convene** to bring together a group of people for a meeting – [26] **irretrievably** in a way that is not possible to correct – [27] **to fuck sth. up** (*phr. v.; offensive*) to damage sth. or do very badly – [28] **formative** (*fml.*) *prägend* – [29] **to succumb to** (*fml.*) here: to accept defeat – [30] **invulnerable** *unverwundbar* – [31] **tide** *Ebbe und Flut*

1. Summarize the excerpt from the novel *The Wall* and point out how the protagonist describes
   a) the country's system of protecting its borders.
   b) the Others.
   c) the societal and economic problems the country/the world is facing.

Step 1:
Read the first two paragraphs of the excerpt and find out what information is given about
- the narrator/the point of view,
- the setting (= time + place),
- the critical situation of the world,
- the Others,
- the Defenders,
- the Wall.

Step 2:
Now read the complete excerpt and subdivide it into paragraphs following the thematic units of the text.

> **Info** »»»
>
> **Paragraphs** subdivide a text into manageable portions and help to organize meaning. Often, each paragraph is organized around a central idea/keyword, which is usually made clear in the first sentence or phrase. However, paragraphs follow each other in a successive order and take the reader from a to b to c, usually linked by connectives or phrases. In a literary text, a new paragraph can indicate:
> - a change of place/time.
> - the introduction of a new character.
> - an interruption of the action.
> - a change in the mode of presentation, e. g. descriptions/explanations given by the narrator (→ panoramic presentation) and monologue/dialogue of the characters (→ scenic presentation).

Tip: Do not only follow the print pattern. If you have difficulties in paragraphing, pay attention to changes and breaks in the course of the narration as described in the Info box above.

Step 3:
SNG-40217-003
Worksheet 3.1
With the help of worksheet 3.1, find a suitable headline for each paragraph, using your notes and your keywords.

Step 4:
SNG-40217-003
Worksheet 3.2
In order to make sure that you have understood everything correctly, use worksheet 3.2 and do the reading comprehension tasks given there.

Step 5:
SNG-40217-003
Worksheet 3.1
Collect relevant information given in the excerpt about these aspects and complete the grid. Use worksheet 3.1 for your notes.

the Change and its effects	the Others and their situation	the Wall	the Defenders	old vs. young
• crops failing • ...	• countries breaking down • ...	• ...	• ...	• none of us could talk • ...

Step 6:
After collecting the most relevant information, write a summary of about 250 words.

Tip: Reactivate your knowledge of how to write a summary and read the respective Skills page in your supplementary booklet (→ Prep Course *kompakt*, p. 62).
Most importantly, use the simple present as your basic tense. Remember to introduce and paraphrase what is said and not simply repeat the text.
Use the phrases given on the page *Vocabulary and Phrases for Text Analysis*, p. 133.

Step 7:
Begin your summary with an introductory sentence that answers the w-questions (who – where – when – what – why) as well as the bibliographical information (author, title, place + time of publishing).

ANALYSIS

2. Examine how the author combines factual information and (personal) opinion and explain its intention and effect on the reader.
   → Prep Course *kompakt*, Analysis of a Fictional Text, p. 18

3. Throughout the whole text, the author creates a situation of 'us and them', referring either to Others vs. Defenders or young vs. old.
   Give examples from the text that emphasize this contrast and explain them.

4. Analyse the author's choice of words* (word fields, positive/negative emotive words) and explain how they underline the particular situation and atmosphere.

ACTIVITIES

5. Imagine you are a reporter working for a national newspaper and your job is to boost morale among the frustrated younger generation.
   Write a newspaper article that shines a positive light on the whole situation of having to serve on the Wall and protecting one's mother country.
   → Prep Course *kompakt*, Writing a Newspaper Article, p. 58

GRAMMAR / LANGUAGE

6. The future British society described by Kavanagh obviously has a lot of strict rules and regulations (*Anweisungen*).
   Make a list of all the regulations mentioned in the excerpt, using **modal auxiliaries** and *if-clauses* (conditional sentences).

   Example:
   - If you belong to the generation born after the Change, you have to serve on the Wall for two years.

   → Appendix, Modal Auxiliaries, p. 116
   → Appendix, Conditional Sentences (If-Clauses), p. 119

7. As described by Kavanagh, most of the young people blame their parents/the older generation for having caused the Change.
   Use different kinds of **if-clauses** (conditional sentences) and write down what the younger generation thinks about their parents and what they wish hadn't happened.

   Examples:
   - If they **hadn't caused** global warming, there **wouldn't have been** any rising sea levels. (type III)
   - If the Others **didn't suffer** from hunger, they **wouldn't attack** us. (type II)

   → Appendix, Conditional Sentences (If-Clauses), p. 119

John Chester
The Biggest Little Farm

AWARENESS

The Biggest Little Farm is a 2018 American environmental documentary film which deals with John Chester's and his wife Molly's realization of their dream. They purchase Apricot Lane Farms in California and leave Los Angeles to re-establish a perfect eco-system in which animals and plants of every kind can co-exist.

Besides John and Molly, the film stars Emma, the pig, and her best friend Mr Greasy, the rooster, along with many other loveable animals.

a) Take a look at the two photos and read the quotations below them.

b) Choose one photo and the quotation that matches your photo best.

c) Team up in groups of four and discuss your choices. Discuss how you understand the quotation and whether you agree or disagree with the understanding of farming given in the quotation and the photo.

Breeding pig Emma and rejected, beat-up rooster Mr Greasy

Piglets playing with each other

The ultimate goal of farming is not the growing of crops[1], but the cultivation and perfection of human beings. *Masanobu Fukunoka*

Farming is a profession of hope. *Brian Brett*

There are two spiritual dangers in not owning a farm. One is the danger of supposing that breakfast comes from the grocery, and the other is that heat comes from the furnace[2]. *Aldo Leopold*

Many years from now, our descendants will look back on the use of animals for food – particularly the intense animal suffering in factory farms – as a moral atrocity[3]. *Jacy Reese*

[1] **crops** grain, fruit or vegetables grown in large amounts – [2] **furnace** *Ofenanlage, Heizkessel* – [3] **atrocity** an extremely cruel, violent and shocking act; *Gräueltat*

27

COMPREHENSION

1. Describe John and Molly Chester's project of establishing a farm in harmony with nature as presented in the trailer to the documentary *The Biggest Little Farm*.

SNG-40217-004
Worksheet 4.1

Step 1:

In order to get an overall understanding of the film and the Chesters' project and intention watch the trailer of the documentary using the link provided on the webcode and do the tasks given on worksheet 4.1.

Step 2:

Watch the trailer **a second time** and answer the questions below in your own words:
- What is John's and Molly's vision of the farm?
- What unexpected challenges and problems did they have to deal with?
- What different kinds of animals and plants are raised and grown on the farm?

Step 3:

A film scene always works on two different levels:
- **the narrative level**, i. e. the story that is told to the viewer
- **the cinematic level**, i. e. the devices that are used to tell the story and turn it into pictures

SNG-40217-004
Worksheet 4.2

Watch the trailer **a third time** and focus on the cinematic devices that are used to convey the particular atmosphere and message of the story. Use worksheet 4.2 and focus on these aspects:
- camera operations   • visual symbols   • film music and sound   • (special) effects
→ Prep Course *kompakt*, Analysis of a Film Scene, p. 20
→ Prep Course *kompakt*, Camera Operations, p. 14

Step 4:

Write a coherent text (about 200 – 250 words) that includes the narrative and cinematic levels of the trailer.

Tip: Remember to write an introductory sentence that contains:
- the title, the type of film and the running time of the film/video clip
- the director's name
- the year of release
- the topic the film deals with
- the important characters

Tips on vocab »»»
- The film depicts the setting of …
- In the first/second … part of the trailer …
- In the introductory/main/concluding part …
- Despite all the problems …
- Eventually, the Chesters have to cope with …
- The film stars animals like … and presents them as …
- Finally, …

Example:

The emotionally gripping trailer of the 2018 documentary *The Biggest Little Farm*, released on YouTube …, deals with …

Step 5:

Use your notes for your description and use connectives to make your writing flow better.
→ Appendix, Connectives and Adverbs, p. 120

ANALYSIS

2. In addition to releasing the trailer, Molly and John Chester gave a lot of interviews to promote not only their film, but also their understanding of sustainable living and farming.
Read the interview with Dave Davies, which focuses particularly on the Chesters' problem with coyotes on the farm.
Illustrate John Chester's solution to the problem by visualizing the vicious circle he was caught in at first – and how he breaks it at last.

Example:

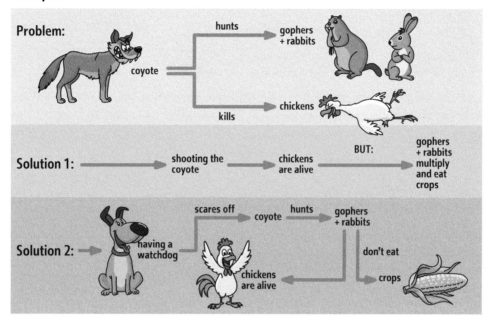

3. Explain John Chester's understanding of the 'job' a farm has to do.

ACTIVITIES

4. Against the background of your results and findings, work creatively and compile your own trailer for a documentary on farming the way you understand it.

SNG-40217-004 @
Worksheet 4.3

Use worksheet 4.3 and work out a storyboard* in which you plan and visualize your film clip.
→ Prep Course *kompakt*, Storyboards and Screenplays, p. 12

Tip: Either use snippets from newspapers or magazines to illustrate your ideas or make rough sketches to visualize characters, setting, visual symbols, etc.

5. The Chesters' (successful) experiment has triggered a controversial debate about the necessity of organic farming, the pollution of the environment through mass animal farming, animal rights, etc.
Put yourself in the position of a (local) politician and prepare a short speech to your constituency (*Wählerschaft*) in which you explain a) your view of the problem and b) possible solutions to the problem.
→ Prep Course *kompakt*, Writing a Speech Script, p. 60

GRAMMAR / LANGUAGE

6. Based on the trailer of *The Biggest Little Farm*, compile a short screenplay* for a documentary about the difference between organic and traditional farming and their environmental impacts. Choose a different genre than the one given, e. g. an eco drama, a sci-fi story, a (tragic/romantic) love story, a thriller, etc.
Before you start:
● Find out about the characteristics of your chosen genre.
● Collect ideas about the plot and possible characters.
● Think about a clear structure for your story.
● Organize your ideas (e. g. in a mind map, a flow chart, etc.).
● Use appropriate language, especially **adjectives, adverbs and emotionally loaded words** to emphasize the character, atmosphere and effect of your chosen genre. Use your dictionary for help.

Examples:

- thriller → gruesome, painful, blood-thirsty, deadly, poisonous, toxic, etc.
- romance → loving, heart-breaking, empathetic, etc.

→ Appendix, Connectives and Adverbs, p. 120
→ Appendix, Adjectives and Adverbs, p. 115

Tip: Use your results of task 4 and worksheet 4.3 for your screenplay. And remember to use the **simple past** as the predominant narrative tense.

Dave Davies

"Biggest Little Farm" Chronicles One Couple's Effort to "Jump-Start the Soil"

Molly and John Chester took a massive leap[1] when they decided to leave Los Angeles to start an organic farm[2]. John's new documentary tells the story of their struggles and successes. [...]

5 The Chesters tried to turn a dry and soil-depleted[3] 200-acre parcel[4] into a lush[5], organic farm. They were determined to tend[6] fruit orchards[7] and raise cows, pigs and chickens in harmony with nature.

Drought[8], pests[9], windstorms and fire threatened to end 10 the venture, but after eight years, their farm, Apricot Lane Farms, is thriving[10]. John Chester, who was a filmmaker before he tried farming, directed a new documentary called "The Biggest Little Farm," about the obstacles[11] he and Molly, a former private chef[12], faced and 15 overcame and what their experiences can tell us about the relationship between humans and our environment. "The Biggest Little Farm" has won several awards at film festivals and will be in theaters this Friday. Molly and John Chester spoke with FRESH AIR's Dave Davies. 20 [...]

DAVIES: This is FRESH AIR. And we're speaking with John and Molly Chester, whose remarkable effort[13] to create a 200-acre biodynamic farm battling[14] droughts, pests and fire is the subject of the new documentary 25 directed by John called "The Biggest Little Farm." While you were still struggling to get the fruit crops going, you were – you had a lot of chickens. And they laid a lot of eggs, and you were able to sell those. So that was really working. But there was a problem with coyotes[15] eating the chickens. How did you try and address that? 30

J CHESTER: Well, the coyotes ate about 350 of our chickens.

DAVIES: Wow.

J CHESTER: And, you know, we refused to shoot the coyote because we wanted to find a way to collaborate[16]. 35 But, you know, ultimately[17], I succumb[18] to it, and I kill a coyote. And I think it's a really important moment in the film because there's something that happens after that that has a profound[19] effect on the way I look at the coyote's role. 40
The coyote also happens to eat gophers[20] and rabbits, another pest on the farm. If we kill all the coyotes, we're going to make that problem worse. And that forced us to find a solution.

DAVIES: It is quite a moment in the film when you 45 shoot the coyote. He's trapped trying to get through a fence, and we can see you level the – looks like a shotgun. What were you thinking then? What were you feeling emotionally?

J CHESTER: In shooting the one coyote, the thing that 50 was weighing on me the most was that I knew this wasn't the only coyote. I was going to have to obliterate[21] every coyote that crossed our path. And we were the farm that had animals, like, that they were eating.

---

[1] **leap** a big change, increase, improvement – [2] **organic farm** Bio-Bauernhof – [3] **soil-depleted** having lost much of its soil – [4] **parcel** (US) an area of land – [5] **lush** with lots of green, healthy plants, grass, etc. – [6] **to tend** (fml.) to care for – [7] **orchard** [ˈɔːtʃəd] Obstgarten – [8] **drought** [draʊt] Dürre – [9] **pest** Schädling, Plage – [10] **to thrive** to grow, develop, be successful – [11] **obstacle** Hindernis – [12] **chef** Koch, Köchin – [13] **effort** Mühe – [14] **to battle** to fight and try hard to achieve sth. – [15] **coyote** [kaɪˈəʊti] – [16] **to collaborate** to work with sb. – [17] **ultimately** finally – [18] **to succumb to** (fml.) to accept defeat – [19] **profound** tiefgreifend – [20] **gopher** Erdhörnchen, Nagetier – [21] **to obliterate** (fml.) to make sth. disappear completely

55 You know, we were creating a food system for coyotes. So it was going to be an endless battle of constantly killing coyotes, and I think that's the thing that scared me the most – was that it felt like an incredibly[22] slippery slope[23]. [...]

60 DAVIES: And then you found a way that the coyotes became helpful. How did that happen?

J CHESTER: Well, after we had shot the one coyote, there was a coyote that ran into the fence of the garden, and it had paralyzed[24] itself. And I had to actually now, 65 you know, euthanize[25] this coyote. It was still alive, but it couldn't move. But when I asked, why is this coyote in the garden? I looked around and it had been digging holes in the garden. It was eating gophers. It was chasing rabbits. It was actually helping to balance another 70 problem. And so I thought, there's got to be another way. And we finally found one of our guardian dogs didn't eat chickens.

DAVIES: (Laughter).

J CHESTER: The only one. Her name was Rosie, and 75 Rosie became the guardian dog of our flock[26]. And, knock on wood[27], we've not lost any chickens since then. So, you know, the coyotes are busy eating, you know, gophers and rabbits.

DAVIES: So the gophers were eating the roots of the 80 fruit trees. That was the problem. And now ...

J CHESTER: Right.

DAVIES: ... That the coyotes can't get the chickens, it goes for the gophers, which is a big help to you.

85 J CHESTER: Yeah. Nature is – they're simple opportunists[28], and you just need to make it slightly harder on one side so that they go the other direction. It sometimes doesn't require as much effort as you think. [...]

DAVIES: You know, to kind of see the process unfold in 90 the movie is really beautiful. You know, we've had a couple of interviews on the show lately about climate change. [...] And I think this film is as inspirational as that can be discouraging, in a way. And it almost makes it hard for me to ask kind of the hard questions, which I do wonder about. Like, can this scale – I mean, can 95 farming this way feed a planet? You know, because we had the Green Revolution in the '60s with all the hybrid seeds[29] and then the monoculture agriculture that does a lot of harm but produces an awful lot of cheap food. I mean, I don't know if you think about it on these terms, 100 but is this a way to feed the planet and change the way we grow food and eat it?

J CHESTER: I think the other way to ask that question is, if we don't start working with our land in a more regenerative[30] way, can the planet feed us? You know, just 105 in the last 260 years, we've destroyed more than a third of the topsoil[31]. We've deforested 46% of the trees. We've doubled CO_2 from 260 to 400 parts per million. We are an incredible force of nature, humans. And we've done all of that unconsciously[32]. And just imagine with con- 110 sciousness[33] for the infinite possibilities of collaboration with nature. Imagine what we could do with that.
I think that charge of a farm to feed the world, you know, comes, like, from post-World War II. It's not the job of a farm to feed the world. It's the job of a farm to 115 feed its community, and the loss of just that understanding is how we got here. Our goal is to feed, you know, the area around us. And yes, is it economically possible? Sure. I mean, not – our way specifically is not the way for every farm, but there's farms that are working in a 120 regenerative way that are economically sustainable[34] – absolutely. And it's just a decision, you know, an act and an understanding of the kinds of farms you're going to support, you know? That's probably going to give us the best chance at a change. 125

DAVIES: Molly Chester, John Chester, thank you so much for spending some time with us. Good luck with the farm, and congratulations on the film.

J CHESTER: Thank you so much.

M CHESTER: Thank you very much. 130

https://www.npr.org/2019/05/06/720697998/biggest-little-farm-chronicles-one-couple-s-effort-to-jump-start-the-soil?t=1563702092029, 6 May 2019 [21.07.2019]

---

[22] **incredibly** extremely – [23] **slippery slope** a bad situation that is likely to get much worse – [24] **to paralyze** lähmen – [25] **to euthanize** ['juːθənaɪz] here: einen Gnadenschuss geben – [26] **flock** a group of birds – [27] **knock on wood** toi toi toi! – [28] **opportunist** sb. that makes the most of a situation; Opportunist – [29] **hybrid seeds** Hybridsaatgut – [30] **regenerative** growing or beginning to grow again – [31] **topsoil** Mutterboden – [32] **unconsciously** unbewusst – [33] **consciousness** Bewusstsein – [34] **sustainable** nachhaltig

Whether it is political speeches, book or film reviews or comments written by journalists, the line between factual information and comment or personal opinion is often unclear. Although reviews especially represent the writer's opinion of a certain publication, it is important to 'read between the lines' and find out about clues given in the text that identify the writer's background and/or his or her attitude to certain topics.

Yolanda Machado
"The Biggest Little Farm" Film Review: Inspirational Farm Tale Avoids Complicated Issues

This gorgeous[1] portrait of a family farm never digs into details about specifics like money, droughts[2] or migrant workers

"The Biggest Little Farm" offers a personal view into one couple's journey in farming and all the trials that come with it, but fails to adequately[3] explore how privilege allowed them to reshape their lives and their farm. [...] Their search led them just an hour outside of Los Angeles to Moorpark. The land they purchased[4] was essentially dead and needed more work than they originally estimated, and with the help of "traditional farming" consultant Alan York, they burned through their first year's budget in just six months.

By focusing on biodiversity – in layman's[5] terms, creating an interlocking[6] ecosystem with a diversity of livestock[7] and crops all supporting each other – the couple started from scratch as Chester filmed the entire process. What followed was several years of ups and downs, of victories and downfalls, and ultimately[8], success and beauty. What the film consistently fails to mention, however, is the cost, selling the story in a subtle[9] "You too can do this!" format. [...]

"The Biggest Little Farm" also only briefly mentions the drought, just as it only fleetingly[10] refers to financial concerns early on. All of these are important issues, ones that farmers need to educate the world about, because it takes more than just a will and some dirt and water to create a successful farm.

In a way, it's misleading to those who view this film as any sort of model to follow, and even more so, it doesn't reach the level of being inspirational because it omits so much of the story. [...]

Still, Chester's experience in filming wildlife and their environments really pays off here. There are some exquisite shots of both the farm and the smallest parts of its ecosystem – the pests[11] and pollinators[12] like bees, butterflies and hummingbirds – that rival any National Geographic film. The use of color and the bird's-eye view shots are particularly stunning, and the before-and-after sequences are truly awe-inspiring[13].

"The Biggest Little Farm" is a decent personal narrative film – even inspiring at times – but it could have provided a much-needed educational view and a deeper look at the importance of California's essential agricultural life.

https://www.thewrap.com/the-biggest-little-farm-film-review-documentary, 9 May 2019 [29.07.2019]

1. You have already dealt with the Chesters' farming experiment in Skill 4.
   a) Read the review above about the film John Chester produced.
   b) Sort the keywords, phrases, adjectives and adverbials which have already been highlighted into the categories in the grid below.
   c) Finally, use the criteria given in the checklist on the opposite page and determine whether the review is positive or negative, biased or objective.

positive	negative	neutral/factual
• inspirational (encouraging)	• avoids (= ignores)	• complicated issues
• …	• but (→ restriction)	• …

2. Having practised with the review on the opposite page, now team up with a partner and examine the review below about John Lanchester's novel *The Wall*, which you dealt with in Skill 3. Use your findings as well as the aspects mentioned in the checklist.

[1] **gorgeous** very beautiful or pleasant – [2] **drought** [draʊt] *Dürre* – [3] **adequately** *angemessen* – [4] **to purchase** (*fml.*) to buy – [5] **layman** *Laie* – [6] **interlocking** closely connected; *ineinandergreifend* – [7] **livestock** animals that are kept on a farm – [8] **ultimately** finally – [9] **subtle** *unterschwellig, subtil* – [10] **fleetingly** in a way that lasts only a short time; *flüchtig* – [11] **pest** *Ungeziefer, Schädling* – [12] **pollinator** *Bestäuber* – [13] **awe-inspiring** *ehrfurchtgebietend*

3. Against the background of your findings, write a review of a film, book or video game of your choice in which you include the aspects mentioned in the checklist.
Remember to flesh out your text with adjectives, adverbials and connectives.
→ Appendix, Connectives and Adverbs, p. 120

Johanna Thomas-Corr
The Wall by John Lanchester – Dystopian Fable for Our Time

The scene is Britain, the time the not-too-distant future. The air hangs heavy with metaphor. Ever since a climatic event known as the "Change", life has, well, changed. Movement between countries is outlawed. There isn't a single beach left anywhere in the world. Britain's coastline has been obliterated[1] by a National Coastal Defence Structure, known to everyone who serves on it as the Wall. Every British youngster is conscripted[2] to spend two years of their life as a "Defender", patrolling 10,000 km of concrete walkways looking for "Others" who might appear at any moment from the sea. Life on the Wall is cold. It is boring. It is utterly[3] grim[4]. [...]

This is the dystopia that John Lanchester has created in his fifth novel, an environmental fable that manages to be both disquieting[5] and quite good fun at the same time. It's a calculated extrapolation[6] of our present anxieties[7] about rising sea levels, anti-refugee populism, post-Brexit scarcity[8] and intergenerational conflict, so day after tomorrow that it's all but guaranteed to be invoked[9] in newspaper columns and kitchen-table debates.

It's hardly a cakewalk[10] for young Defenders such as Kavanagh, whose conscription begins at a point of national crisis. Others are marauding[11] in "big numbers, dangerous numbers" (more than 94) according to a politician (known as "the blond baby") who visits the troops to deliver platitudinous[12] pep talks[13]. It comes as no surprise that the young are disgusted by "the olds". They are responsible for the Change but have never done time on the Wall, which is, as Kavanagh says, "the single most important and informative experience in the lives of my generation". When he visits his parents, they can't look him in the eye, ashamed that the world "broke on their watch". [...]

Lanchester reveals with slow, steady control the cruelties of his strange new world. [...]

So why, then, is *The Wall* a little unsatisfying? One problem is that it's not nearly strange enough – the ambient[14] unease rarely trickles down[15] to a human level. [...] Despite being very different to Lanchester's last novel, *Capital, The Wall* suffers from some of the same flaws[15]: underdeveloped characters, particularly the women, a lack of convincing detail and an overly schematic plot. [...]

The Wall feels a bit basic by comparison. But it's resolutely[17] British at least – and you can't help wondering if it's the dystopia our lonely, windswept[18] islands deserve.

https://www.theguardian.com/books/2019/jan/15/the-wall-by-john-lanchester-review, 15 January 2019 [01.08.2019]

Checklist

Clues given ...	... indicate ...
• the writer's (professional/personal) interest and neutrality	→ professionality and credibility
• background, medium and source where the text is published (public/private, NGO, political, etc.)	→ neutrality or personal/professional interest
• choice of words (positive/negative, emotive, neutral)	→ neutrality or bias
• supporting facts and references; quality of sources, e.g. cartoons, statistical data	→ reliability
• statements and conclusions (based on evidence or assumption)	→ neutrality, professionality
• use of language (formal, informal, disapproving)	→ neutrality or bias
• use of irony, exaggeration, superlatives	→ neutrality or bias
• clear distinction between fact and fiction	→ clarity and factuality
• use of (strong, judgmental) adjectives and adverbials	→ wielding influence and showing emotion

[1] **to obliterate** (*fml.*) *auslöschen, ausradieren* – [2] **to conscript** to force sb. by law to serve in the armed forces – [3] **utterly** completely, extremely – [4] **grim** worrying, without hope – [5] **disquieting** (*fml.*) causing worry – [6] **extrapolation** *Weiterführung* – [7] **anxiety** [æŋˈzaɪəti] fear, concern – [8] **scarcity** *Knappheit* – [9] **to invoke** (*fml.*) *aufrufen* – [10] **cakewalk** (*infml.*) *Kinderspiel* – [11] **to maraud** *plündern* – [12] **platitudinous** (*fml.*) boring and having no meaning – [13] **pep talk** *aufmunternde Worte* – [14] **ambient** *allgegenwärtig* – [15] **to trickle down** *nach unten durchsickern* – [16] **flaw** weakness, fault – [17] **resolutely** (*fml.*) *entschlossen* – [18] **windswept** *windumtost*

Growing Up –
No Longer Being a Child!

A Child No More by Christopher Weyant, 21 February 2018, in: The Boston Globe

Tips on vocab »»»

to hide behind sth. ▪ to tip over (*umkippen*) ▪ things lying around ▪ the Capitol building (Washington D. C.) ▪ demonstrators ▪ to protest/demonstrate against sb./sth. ▪ to hold up placards ▪ masses of people ▪ backpackers

START-UP ACTIVITIES

"I can't see you, [therefore] you can't see me" expresses a typical way of thinking and behaviour of pre-school children – without eye contact, you are invisible. According to their understanding, it is impossible to see the other, unless two people make eye contact. In 2017, research by developmental psychologists of the University of Southern California revealed
5 that children have a "we" perspective – they demand reciprocity and mental engagement between individuals. Thus, children feel unable to relate to a person unless the (non-verbal and verbal) communication flows both ways, because they cannot distinguish clearly between the "I" and "you" perspective yet.

 1. Team up with a partner and describe the two situations depicted in the cartoon above.
→ Prep Course *kompakt*, Analysis of Visuals, p. 30

Miley Cyrus
Inspired

I'm writing down my dreams, all I'd like to see
Starting with the bees or else they're gonna die
There won't be no[1] trees or air for us to breathe
I'll start feeling mad, but then I feel inspired
5 Thinking about the days coming home with dirty feet
From playing with my dad all day in the creek[2]
He somehow has a way of knowing what to say
So when I'm feeling sad, he makes me feel inspired

We are meant for more
10 You're the handle on the door that opens up to change
I know that sounds so strange, to think
We are meant for more
Pull the handle on the door that opens up to change
I know that sounds so strange
15 'Cause you've always felt so small, but know you aren't at all
And I hope you feel inspired
Oh, I hope you feel inspired

How can we escape all the fear and all the hate?
Is anyone watching us down here?
20 Death is life, it's not a curse[3]
Reminds us of time and what it's worth
To make the most out of it while we're here

We are meant for more
Pull the handle on the door that opens up to change
25 I know it sounds so strange
We are meant for more
There's a lock[4] upon the door, but we hold the key to change

But how can we escape all the fear and all the hate?
Is anyone watching us down here?

2. Relate the statement "I put away childish things", made in the cartoon, to the short text underneath. What happens if there is no "reciprocity" when you are a child – and later, when you are a teenager?

 3. In a paired reading/listening activity, find examples in the song that reveal how the speaker overcomes fear, hate and sadness and finds inspiration and opportunities of change.
→ Prep Course *kompakt*, Analysis of Poetry and Lyrics, p. 24

---

[1] **there won't be no** (*infml.*) there won't be any – [2] **creek** a stream or narrow river; *Flüsschen* – [3] **curse** *Fluch* – [4] **lock** *(Tür-)Schloss*

Jennifer Clement

Gun Love

The photograph below shows Slab City ("The Slabs") in the Sonoran Desert, the so-called California Badlands, approximately 170 miles southeast of Los Angeles. The Slabs is a compound owned by the state of California which is inhabited by ca. 150 permanent residents all year round. Many of them are dependent on social benefit and homeless and live in abandoned trailers or self-made shacks. The site has no electricity, running water, sanitary installations like sewers or toilets, or garbage removal services. The name Slabs derives from concrete slabs that were left behind after a WW II Marine Corps barracks was abandoned.

In a Round Robin-activity, describe the impression the community makes on you. What do you consider people's lives to be like?

In the 2018 novel *Gun Love*, the 14-year-old protagonist, Pearl, describes her and her mother's life in a trailer park in Florida that has gone to rack and ruin over time.

Me? I was raised in a car and, when you live in a car, you're not worried about storms and lightning, you're afraid of a tow truck[1].

My mother and I moved into the Mercury[2] when she was seventeen and I was newborn. So our car, at the edge[3] of a trailer park[4] in the middle of Florida, was the only home I ever knew. We lived a dot-to-dot life[5], never thinking too much about the future.

The old car had been bought for my mother on her sixteenth birthday.

The 1994 Mercury Topaz automatic had once been red but was now covered in several coats[6] of white from my

[5] (line marker)

[10] (line marker)

---

[1] **tow truck** *Abschleppwagen* – [2] **Mercury** an entry-level car brand, produced by the Ford Motor company; defunct in 2011 – [3] **at the edge** the outer point of sth. – [4] **trailer park** an area of ground where mobile homes can be parked, esp. by people using them as their homes – [5] **a dot-to-dot life** a form of drawing in which numbered dots on a page must be connected in ascending order to create a final picture – [6] **coat** here: a layer

mother painting the car every few years as if it were a house. The red paint still appeared under scratches and
15 scrapes. Out the front window was a view of the trailer park and a large sign that read: WELCOME TO INDIAN WATERS TRAILER PARK.

Our car was turned off under a sign that said Visitors Parking. My mother thought we'd only be there for a
20 month or two, but we stopped there for fourteen years. Once in a while when people asked my mother what is was like to live in a car, she answered, You're always looking for a shower.

The only thing we ever really worried about was CPS,
25 Child Protective Services[7], coming around. My mother was afraid that someone at my school or her job might think they should call the abuse hotline on her and take me off to a foster home[8].

She knew the acronyms that were like the rest-in-peace
30 letters on tombstones: CPSL, Child Protective Services Law; FCP, Foster Care Plus; and FF, Family Finding[9].

We can't go around making too many friends, my mother said. There's always some person who wants to be a saint and sit on a chair in heaven. A friend can become
35 Your Honor[10] in an instant.

Since when is living in a car something you can call abuse? she asked without expecting me to answer.

The park was located in Putnam County[11]. The land had been cleared to hold at least fifteen trailers, but there
40 were only four trailers that were occupied. My friend April May lived in one with her parents, Rose and Sergeant Bob. Pastor Rex inhabited one all by himself while Mrs. Roberta Young and her adult daughter Noelle occupied one right next to the dilapidated[12] recreation ar-
45 ea[13]. A Mexican couple, Corazón and Ray, lived in a trailer toward the back of the park, far from the entrance and our car.

We were not in the south of Florida near the warm beaches and the Gulf of Mexico. We were not near the
50 orange groves[14] or too close to St. Augustine, the oldest city in America. We were not near the Everglades[15], where clouds of mosquitos and a thick canopy[16] of vines protected delicate orchids[17]. Miami, with its sounds of Cuban music and streets filled with convertibles, was a
55 long drive. Animal Kingdom and the Magic Kingdom were miles away. We were nowhere.

Two highways and a creek, which we all called a river but was only a small stream off the St. John's, surrounded the trailer park. The town dump was at the back
60 through some trees. We breathed in the garbage. We breathed in gas of rot and rust, corroded batteries, decomposing food, deadly hospital waste, odors of medicines and clouds of cleaning chemicals.

My mother said, Who would clear land for a trailer park
65 and a garbage dump on a sacred Indian ground? This land belongs to the Timucua tribes and their spirits are everywhere. If you plant a seed, something else grows. If you plant a rose, a carnation[18] comes out of the ground. If you plant a lemon tree, this earth will give
70 you a palm tree. If you plant a white oak, a tall man will grow. The ground here is puzzled.

My mother was right. In our part of Florida everything was puzzled. Life was always like shoes on the wrong foot.

75 When I read over the headlines on the newspapers that were lined up at the checkout counter at the local store beside the gum and candy, I knew Florida was asking for something. I read: DON'T CALL 911[19] BUY A GUN; BEAR RETURNS TO CITY AFTER BEING RELOCAT-
80 ED; DEADLY MEXICAN HEROIN KILLS FOUR; and HURRICANE BECOMES A CLOUDY DAY.

from *Gun Love* by Jennifer Clement. Hogarth Press, London, 2018, pp. 3 ff.

COMPREHENSION

1. In a paired reading activity,
- read the excerpt on your own first,
- then point out the overall situation that is depicted there to your partner.

Try to answer the w-questions (who – what – where – when – why) and clarify unknown vocabulary and further questions.

---

[7] **Child Protective Services** US governmental agency responsible for the protection and care of children – [8] **foster home** *Pflegefamilie* –
[9] **Family Finding** national US organization helping to connect children with a family – [10] **Your Honor** (*fml.*) title of respect when speaking to a judge; *Euer Ehren!* – [11] **Putnam County** county in northeastern Florida – [12] **dilapidated** old and in poor condition – [13] **recreation area** area to relax and enjoy yourself – [14] **orange grove** *Orangenhain* – [15] **Everglades** US national park; a network of wetlands and forests – [16] **canopy** *Baldachin* – [17] **orchid** [ˈɔːkɪd] *Orchidee* – [18] **carnation** *Nelke* – [19] **911** the phone number used in the US to call the emergency services; *110*

2. After reading the text a second time, do the reading comprehension tasks on worksheet 5.1 to get a more detailed understanding of the situation depicted in the excerpt.

SNG-40217-005
Worksheet 5.1

3. Write a summary of about 150–200 words, pointing out briefly what the text is about.

Tip: Remember to begin your summary with an introductory sentence that answers the w-questions. Be careful to use the present tense in your text.

Example:
In the given excerpt from the novel *Gun Love*, published in 2018, the 14-year-old protagonist and the first-person narrator of the novel, Pearl, describes …
→ Prep Course *kompakt*, Writing a Summary, p. 62

ANALYSIS

4. Examine the narrative and metaphorical devices* employed in the text and explain how they support
a) the message of the text,
b) the overall atmosphere,
c) the implicit (= not directly expressed) nightmare Pearl experiences.

Tip: Before you start working with the stylistic details in the text, make sure that you have understood the complex task. Pay attention to the **keywords in the assignment**, which show you what to focus on and what exactly you are expected to examine and explain. Pay particular attention to the standardized terminology (*Operatoren*).
→ Standardized Terminology, pp. 8 ff.

Info 》》

- **Imagery** words that appeal to the readers' senses, e. g. sights, sounds, etc.
- **Allusions** are indirect references to e. g. a famous event, a person or a well-known piece of literature.
- An **allegory** is a text that may be understood on a superficial or factual level and a deeper, more philosophical level that requires you to use your background knowledge and read between the lines.
- A **simile** is a comparison using *like* or *as*.
- A **metaphor** is a poetic comparison without using *like* or *as* (e. g. an ocean of tears).
- A **symbol** is sth. concrete that stands for sth. abstract (e. g. cross – Christianity)

Info 》》

Narrative technique/narrative perspective:
- **point of view:** the perspective from which the characters or events are presented
- **unlimited point of view/omniscient narrator:** a narrator who knows everything; present the action and the characters' thoughts, etc.
- **limited point of view:** e. g. a first-person narrator who only has limited insight
- **witness/observer narrator:** a narrator who is a character in the story (e. g. protagonist or minor character); usually has a limited perspective
- **stream of consciousness:** the presentation of experiences and thoughts through the mind (→ thoughts) of one character in a text (→ *erlebte Rede*); a special technique here is the interior monologue (a special kind of scenic presentation which is often not ordered or logical)
- **mode of presentation:**
  a) panoramic → the narrator tells the story
  b) scenic → the narrator shows an event in detail using dialogue and describing a scene, etc.

Step 1:

Using the clues given in the assignment and your notes from tasks 1 and 2, collect information about Pearl and the circumstances of her life.

Juxtapose (= *gegenüberstellen*) Pearl's remarks and descriptions with what you think is really meant and expressed.

Pearl's remarks/descriptions	implied meaning
• I was raised in a car … • My mother and I moved into the Mercury when she was seventeen and I was newborn. • … • …	→ Pearl has been homeless all her life → …

SNG-40217-005
Worksheet 5.2 You can use worksheet 5.2 for your detailed notes.

→ Prep Course *kompakt*, Analysis of a Fictional Text, p. 18

Step 2:

Exchange and compare your findings in class and make additions and corrections to your notes if necessary.

Step 3:

In the given excerpt, the narrator particularly makes use of contrast (antithesis*) when talking about

- Florida,
- the trailer park,
- the 1994 Mercury Topaz automatic,
- the sacred Indian ground.

SNG-40217-005
Worksheet 5.3 Use worksheet 5.3 and try to explain the function and meaning of these contrasts.

Step 4:

Reactivate your knowledge of stylistic devices*, metaphors* and imagery using the info box on p. 38 and the respective pages in the Prep Course *kompakt* booklet.

→ Appendix, Literary Terms, p. 135

Step 5:

Explain the function of the devices listed below using examples from the text.

- contrast (antithesis*)
- symbol*
- simile*
- wordfield(s*)
- allusion*
- parallelism/anaphora*
- rhetorical question*

SNG-40217-005
Worksheet 5.4 You can use the grid provided on worksheet 5.4 for your notes.

Step 6:

Against the background of your findings and analysis results, draw conclusions about the message of the text.

Tip: Focus on relevant topics/aspects of the text and do not get sidetracked by too many details.

- What is (implicitly) said about homelessness?
- What is said about living in a trailer park (e. g. poverty, etc.)?
- What kind of people live in the trailer park?
- What overall atmosphere does the excerpt convey?

Step 7:

Finally, using all your notes and considerations, explain how the narrative perspective* and the stylistic devices* support the message of the text. Write a coherent text of about 350 words and use the 'introduction – main part – conclusion' pattern for your text.

→ Prep Course *kompakt*, Writing an Analysis, p. 48

5. The text at hand, taken from a novel, describes a serious topic through the eyes of a 14-year-old girl, who appears to be quite content and at ease with her situation. However, in real life, homelessness and particularly the homelessness of youth – or even worse, parenting youth (= teenage mothers/fathers) – has become a sad reality for many young people.

Take a look at the map and the tables below, which are taken from the *2018 Annual Homelessness Assessment Report to Congress*, and state the striking/peak numbers given there. Which overall trends can you detect?

→ Prep Course *kompakt*, Analysis of Statistical Data, p. 28

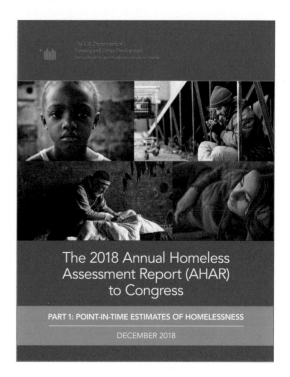

The 2018 Annual Homeless Assessment Report (AHAR) to Congress

PART 1: POINT-IN-TIME ESTIMATES OF HOMELESSNESS

DECEMBER 2018

Estimates of Homeless People
By State, 2018

Number of People Experiencing Homelessness per 10,000 People

- Less than 10
- 10–24
- 25–49
- 50+

Parenting Youth
By Sheltered Status, 2018

	People in Parenting Youth Families		Sheltered People in Parenting Youth Families		Unsheltered People in Parenting Youth Families	
	Number	Percent	Number	Percent	Number	Percent
Total	8,724	100 %	88,249	100 %	475	100 %
Parenting Youth (Under 18)	87	1.0 %	77	0.9 %	10	2.1 %
Parenting Youth (18 to 24)	8,637	99.0 %	88,172	99.1 %	465	97.9 %
Children of Parenting Youth	11,319		10,791		528	

Demographic Characteristics of Homeless People in Families with Children
2018

Characteristics	All Homeless People in Families		Sheltered People in Families		Unsheltered People in Families	
	#	%	#	%	#	%
People in Families	180,413	100 %	164,023	100 %	16,390	100 %
Age						
Under 18	107,301	59.5 %	98,903	60.3 %	8,398	51.2 %
18 – 24	14,187	7.9 %	12,688	7.7 %	1,499	9.1 %
Over 24	58,925	32.7 %	52,432	32.0 %	6,493	39.6 %
Gender						
Female	109,340	60.6 %	100,842	61.5 %	8,498	51.8 %
Male	70,900	39.3 %	63,110	38.5 %	7,790	47.5 %
Transgender	75	0.0 %	44	0.0 %	31	0.2 %
Gender Non-conforming	98	0.1 %	27	0.0 %	71	0.4 %
Ethnicity						
Non-Hispanic/Latino	128,360	71.1 %	115,721	70.6 %	12,639	77.1 %
Hispanic/Latino	52,053	28.9 %	48,302	29.4 %	3,751	22.9 %
Race						
White	68,522	38.0 %	58,901	35.9 %	9,621	58.7 %
Black or African American	91,068	50.5 %	87,745	53.5 %	3,323	20.3 %
Asian	1,724	1.0 %	1,412	0.9 %	312	1.9 %
Native American	3,602	2.0 %	3,077	1.9 %	525	3.2 %
Pacific Islander	3,911	2.2 %	2,561	1.6 %	1,350	8.2 %
Multiple Races	11,586	6.4 %	10,327	6.3 %	1,259	7.7 %

HUD Exchange/The U.S. Department of Housing and Urban Development: The 2018 Annual Homelessness Assessment Report (AHAR) to Congress

GRAMMAR / LANGUAGE ⟩⟩⟩⟩⟩⟩

6. Imagine you work for an NGO that wants to help and support teenage mothers, run-away children and homeless youth. That means you have to **conduct interviews** with people like Pearl and her mother to get a full picture of their living conditions and needs.

Write down possible **questions** that make the interview partners talk.

Info ⟩⟩⟩

1) **yes-no question** → Do you feel safe?
2) **open question** → What made you and your mom stay here?
3) **question after statement** → There has been a rumour about serious problems … what actually went wrong?
4) **question referring back** → The other inhabitants in the trailer park mentioned … How do you view …?
5) **confrontational question** → What do you tell people when they call you losers?
6) **indirectly expressed question** → Well, I thought you might be interested in giving us an overview of ….

Additionally, employ **modal auxiliaries** to phrase things politely and not offend or intimidate your interview partners.

→ Appendix, Modal Auxiliaries, p. 116

Examples:

- You said, you and your mom live in a car … which is your home … could you tell us how it feels to live in a car?
- Without going into too much detail now, how would you describe your living conditions here in the trailer park?

 Finally, act out the interviews in class and think about possible answers the interviewees might give.

Nosheen Iqbal

Generation Z: 'We Have More to Do than Drink and Take Drugs'

AWARENESS

Demographers[1] and researchers usually use birth years, ranging from the early 20th century until today, to identify and categorize generational characteristics and developments/trends.
Do research and find information about these major generations:

- Lost Generation
- Greatest Generation
- Silent Generation
- Baby Boomers
- Generation X
- Millennials
- Generation Z

1 They drink less, take far fewer drugs and have made teenage pregnancy a near anomaly[2]. Generation Z – one of several terms used to describe post-millennial youth born after 1996 – prefer juice bars to pub crawls[3],
5 rank quality family time ahead of sex and prioritise good grades before friendship, at least according to a report published by the British Pregnancy Advisory Service last week.
An onslaught[4] of sneering[5] headlines followed, charac-
10 terising today's youth as boring, sensible and hopelessly screen-addicted.
So, are the kids all right?
"We have so much more to do than [just] drink and take drugs," says Demi Babalola, a 19-year-old philosophy
15 and sociology student. "I'm not surprised those [statistics] show that's the case: it makes sense. We have a lot more to distract[6] us now."
What's her biggest time stealer? "Social media." Babalola toggles between[7] Snapchat, Twitter and Instagram,
20 although she rolls her eyes at the mention of Facebook, full as it is of "older people".
But it's not just the breadth[8] of entertainment and culture that is so instantly available – and disposable[9] – to Babalola and her peers. There is also a growing feeling
25 that the preoccupations[10] of her parents' generation seem, well, a bit lame.
"Going out takes a lot of effort: it's boring, repetitive and expensive," she says. "Obviously, I used to go out a lot in my first year [at university], but now we do more kickbacks[11]."
30 [...]

2 The cliché that many young people spend far too much time online, instead of indulging in[12] a romanticised form of rebellion, may have some truth, but as futurologist Rhiannon McGregor points out, Gen Z-ers
35 are more cautious[13] and risk-averse[14] than their parents, partly because that technology exists.
"They're aware from an early age of how they're portrayed online and offline, so they curate[15] themselves in a more conservative way," she says. (In other words, no
40 one wants to be publicly shamed getting messy or being recklessly[16] daft[17].)
"But they're also more socially aware and see themselves as part of a global community. It's easier to get and feel connected to someone in Africa or Asia and
45 share concerns about climate change, for instance."

3 Clara Finnigan, 22, who grew up in Devon and is in her final year at the University of Arts London, points out that one size doesn't fit all. She still goes out, "often to gay clubs".
50 She believes her generation is unfairly judged and that it reports levels of stress and depression that are higher than ever because of the economic and political state of the world it has inherited[18].
"The whole anxiety[19] of not having stability in your fu-
55 ture is something that is definitely very present. I won't

---

[1] **demographer** [dɪˈmɒɡrəfər] *Bevölkerungskundler/-in, Demograf* – [2] **anomaly** (*fml.*) sth. that is different from what is usual – [3] **pub crawl** *Kneipentour* – [4] **onslaught** very powerful attack – [5] **to sneer** *spöttisch grinsen* – [6] **to distract** *ablenken* – [7] **to toggle between** to switch a feature on a tablet or mobile phone on and off by pressing the same button – [8] **breadth** [bredθ] *Breite* – [9] **disposable** intended to be thrown away after use – [10] **preoccupation** the thing you think about most – [11] **kickback** small gathering of a group of friends – [12] **to indulge in** *jdm./etw. nachgeben* – [13] **cautious** avoiding risks, careful – [14] **risk-averse** unwilling to take risks – [15] **to curate** to select things such as documents, music, products or internet content to be included as part of a list or collection, or on a website – [16] **reckless** *rücksichtslos* – [17] **adrift** aimless – [18] **to inherit** *erben* – [19] **anxiety** [æŋˈzaɪəti] fear, worry

probably ever own my own house, unless I get really lucky."

She slumps[20] in her seat at the pretentiously[21] swanky[22] bar we meet in. "I just want what previous generations have had: you work hard, you reap the rewards[23] of that. Sometimes I feel a bit hopeless because [my degree and hard work] won't make a difference.

"I don't expect to have one full-time gig[24]; my career won't be defined by one job. I know I'll have to do stuff I don't enjoy to be able to do passion projects that I do."

4 Amelia Colthart, a 22-year-old graduate from Leicester, and Myesha Owen Munro, a 17-year-old A-level student from north London, both agree.

"At my age, my parents and my grandparents owned their own home," says Colthart. "I don't go out clubbing[25] – I know my limits. I go to friends' houses [for kickbacks], but I have to prioritise my career goals because it's a lot harder to achieve what I want."

Owen Munro adds: "My generation feels bitter about all the things we won't be able to do because of what the older generation chose."

The subjects of Brexit and of dropping out of university to pursue[26] less mind-bogglingly[27] expensive apprenticeships[28] come up a lot. As does a consistent refusal[29] to accept that anyone should be defined by traditional markers of identity.

"We're more inclusive[30]," says Babalola. "You can do what you want as long as you don't harm anyone and stay safe. It's about freedom. Previous generations always made distinct[31] separations between being gay or straight. [...]

While statistics show that smoking, drinking and clubbing may be in decline for today's young people, the health and wellness industry is booming with the same demographic – in part, because these young people have had so much information at their disposal[32].

"The risks and downsides of doing all of those things have been drummed into[33] us at school from an early age," says Colthart. "Self-care is a much bigger deal for us."

5 Generation Z-ers will, after all, be living longer and more healthily, and looking better for it.

A report (pdf) from the Institute of Alcohol Studies suggests that changing demographics also play a part, reporting that "ethnic minority children ... are less likely to drink, [which] can directly explain a small proportion of the fall in underage drinking" but also that there is evidence these same minority students can also influence their peers. [...]

So what is the new going out? The Generation Z idea of fun that is inexplicable[34] to older adults? Owen Munro, Allely and Babalola instantly refer me to Snapchat, where they communicate in a constant group feed with their friends. Broadcasting the minutiae[35] of her day – a good outfit, a trip to Westfield – is as second nature[36] as breathing to Babalola.

"It's kind of documenting your life, but you have an audience and you immediately know who's interacting. I enjoy it – it makes me feel important that 100 people are watching what I'm eating."

"It's easier than Instagram," agrees Owen Munro. "I hate putting up a picture and waiting to see if anyone likes it. It's scary."

And what are Babalola's plans for today? "My friends and I go out to London, or cycling. We might go to a cute cafe and take pictures."

https://www.theguardian.com/society/2018/jul/21/generation-z-has-different-attitudes-says-a-new-report, 21 July 2018 [22.08.2019]

COMPREHENSION ⟫⟫⟫⟫

1. Give an outline of the article and say what it writes about
- the general attitude of Generation Z.
- Generation Z's
   a) likes and dislikes, b) concerns and anxieties, c) plans for the future, d) handling of social media.

Write a coherent text of about 200 – 250 words.

[20] **to slump** to sit or fall heavily and suddenly – [21] **pretentious** trying to give the appearance of great importance – [22] **swanky** (*infml.*) very expensive and stylish – [23] **to reap the rewards of sth.** *den Erfolg von etw. ernten* – [24] **gig** (*infml.*) a job – [25] **to go out clubbing** to go out dancing in clubs – [26] **to pursue** to try to achieve a plan over a long period of time – [27] **mind-boggling** (*infml.*) extremely surprising and difficult to understand or imagine – [28] **apprenticeship** *Ausbildung, Lehre* – [29] **refusal** *Weigerung* – [30] **inclusive** determined to include many different types of people and treat them all fairly and equally – [31] **distinct** clearly noticeable – [32] **at sb.'s disposal** (*fml.*) available to be used by sb. – [33] **to drum sth. into sb.** *in jdn. hineinhämmern* – [34] **inexplicable** [ˌɪn.ɪkˈsplɪkəbəl] unable to be explained or understood – [35] **the minutiae** [mɪˈnuːʃiaɪ] small and often unimportant details – [36] **second nature** sth. that is so familiar that it is done without having to think about it, natural

M **2.** Team up with a partner, and mediate and describe the bar charts on pp. 45 f. depicting
- Generation Z's attitude toward social responsibility and the protection of the environment.
- Generation Z's criteria for shopping textiles.
→ Prep Course *kompakt*, Analysis of Statistical Data, p. 28

ANALYSIS ⟫⟫⟫

3. Analyse the structural and stylistic devices* of the article and determine its credibility.

Step 1:

Identify the train of thought/line of argument in the article as well as its compositional patterns. Draw a flowchart to visualize your findings.

Example:

Introduction of report/ general characteristics … ⟩	… reaction to … ⟩	… question: … ⟩
⟩	Example: Demi Babalola … ⟩	⟩
Report … ⟩	⟩	Conclusion: … ⟩

Info ⟫⟫⟫

> **Structural devices** are used to organize and structure a text and guide the reader through it. Here are some commonly used structural devices:
> - **column** (*Textspalte*)
> - a **heading/headline** used to arouse the reader's interest
> - a **conclusion** often re-states the main idea and summarizes the main aspects of the text
> - the **introduction** leads into the topic, attracts the reader's interest or draws her or him into the story
> - **main part:** the topic/problem is demonstrated and the intention/problem is discussed
> - **paragraph:** a division of text dealing with a particular idea
> - **subheading:** a caption that divides the text into logical sections
> - **line of argument(ation):** the way different reasons are gradually developed to convince a reader of a particular point of view
> - **train of thought:** the way a series of ideas is gradually developed and structured

Step 2:

In a further step, focus on stylistic devices* the author employs in order to emphasize the line of argument*. Pay particular attention to these devices, sort them in a grid and explain their function. Use worksheet 6.1 for detailed notes.

SNG-40217-006
Worksheet 6.1

device	example from the text	function	message
enumeration	… drink less, take … fewer drugs and have made …	→ emphasis on correctness → anti-climax (fewer, less …)	→ this generation is very different → they behave very correctly
positive vs. negative emotive words	…	→ …	→ …
keywords	…	→ …	→ …

→ Prep Course *kompakt*, Analysis of a Non-Fictional Text, p. 22
→ Appendix, Literary Terms, p. 135

Step 3:

After completing the grid, write a coherent text of about 300 words in which you explain the author's line of argu-ment* and the message of the text. Be careful to quote from the article to prove the accuracy and correctness of your analysis.

→ Prep Course *kompakt*, Analysis of a Non-Fictional Text, p. 22

Tip: Make sure to employ connectives and linkers to make your text flow better.

→ Appendix, Connectives and Adverbs, p. 120

Tips on vocab »»

- The author describes the characteristics of …
- The writer makes an allusion to …
- The author's train of thought is under-lined by …
- The intention of the author is to …
- At the beginning of the article …
- The main/principal idea is that …
- In the main/final part, the author …
- The author raises the question if …
- The author/article relates to …

Tips on vocab »»

to begin with ■ to start with ■ furthermore/moreover ■ generally speaking ■ in comparison to ■ in contrast ■ therefore ■ as a matter of fact ■ according to ■ seemingly

---

ACTIVITIES »»»»»»

4. Your American friend Jasmine is doing a project on 'Generation Z' in her social sciences class. In an e-mail, she asks you if you can help her with further material on the matter.

You have come across the bar charts below/on page 46 in the online version of the German newspaper *Die Welt*, which show the contradictory shopping habits of Generation Z.

In an e-mail, tell your friend about the bar charts and give her the most relevant information in English about the core aspects regarding Generation Z's attitude towards:

- environment and sustainability
- social values
- fashion and shopping

→ Prep Course *kompakt*, Mediation, p. 36

Das widersprüchliche Kaufverhalten der Generation Z

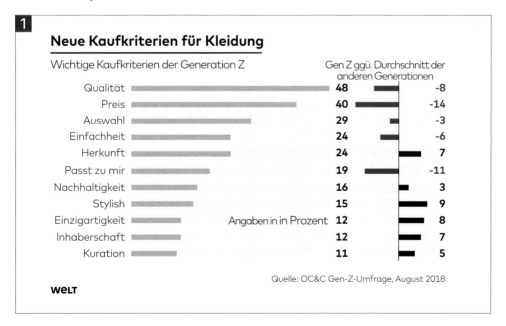

1

Neue Kaufkriterien für Kleidung

Wichtige Kaufkriterien der Generation Z

Gen Z ggü. Durchschnitt der anderen Generationen

Qualität	48	-8
Preis	40	-14
Auswahl	29	-3
Einfachheit	24	-6
Herkunft	24	7
Passt zu mir	19	-11
Nachhaltigkeit	16	3
Stylish	15	9
Einzigartigkeit	12	8
Inhaberschaft	12	7
Kuration	11	5

Angaben in in Prozent

Quelle: OC&C Gen-Z-Umfrage, August 2018

WELT

Soziale Verantwortung vor Umweltschutz

Vollständige Verpflichtung zu folgenden Aussagen in Prozent

■ Umwelt   ■ Soziale Verantwortung   ■ Ethik / Sonstiges

Unterschied zum Durchschnitt der **vorigen** Generationen

Aussage	Prozent	Unterschied
Engagement für den Tierschutz	23	−0,1
Gewährleistung, dass meine Familie gute Chancen hat	22	−9,1
Reduzierung meiner Klimabilanz	18	3,3
Sicherheit meiner Nachbarschaft	17	6,1
Kauf von Produkten auf Grundlage der Nachhaltigkeit / ethischen Merkmale	17	4,4
Reduzierung meines Abfallaufkommens	16	−8,6
Beitrag zur Stärkung lokaler Gemeinden	15	5,0
Bekämpfung von Ungleichheit in der Gesellschaft	15	4,6
Unterstützung von Menschenrechts-organisationen	14	2,3
Vielfalt am Arbeitsplatz / Bildungsinstitut	13	4,2
Reduzierung des Verbrauchs an Einweg-Plastik	11	−13,4

WELT

Quelle: OC&C Gen Z Survey, August 2018

GRAMMAR / LANGUAGE

5. Write a letter to the editor in which you state your view on the matter. Employ **gerund and participle constructions** to vary your style and way of expressing your ideas.

Examples:
- Feeling bitter about what the older generation was able to do … widens the gap …
- Instead of openly rebelling against injustices, Gen Z prefers to …

6. Turn the language and phrases in the box below into everyday English.

Example:
- post-millennial youth → sb. born after the year 2000

> screen-addicted ● peers ● global community ● markers of identity ● wellness industry ●
> to prioritize ● demographic ● WhatsApp ● face-to-face interaction

The Duke of Sussex (Prince Harry)
The Power of the Invisible Role Model

The Duke of Sussex, better known as Prince Harry, is the second son of Charles, Prince of Wales, and Diana, Princess of Wales. After years of trying to come to terms with his mother's death, and serving in the British army, he finally seems to have found his role in life. In 2014, he launched the *Invictus Games*, a paralympic-style sport event, which he – along with numerous non-profit organizations and charities – also patrons. Prince Harry particularly supports the empowerment of youth, the preservation of (African) wildlife and nature as well as injured servicemen and -women and veterans of war. In May 2018, he married the African-American actress Meghan Markle, and their first child, Archie Mountbatten-Windsor, was born in May 2019.

Everybody has (had) certain role models in life, whether they are famous celebrities, public figures or just 'everyday' people. Reflect on what you consider to be relevant characteristics of a person that make them role models for others. Pick 3 – 5 traits from the box below and explain why they are most important to you.

confidence ● leadership ● courage ● concern ● uniqueness ● communication ● respect ● humility ● knowledge ● well-roundedness ● doing good things ● willingness to admit mistakes ● passion ● inspiring others ● having a clear set of values ● commitment ● selflessness ● tolerance ● trust ● overcoming obstacles ● integrity ● ambition ● success ● efforts to improve ● creativity ● optimism ● hardworking ● empathizing ● sincerity ● generosity ● determination ● joy ● love ● positivity ● responsibility ● persistence	

Webcode SNG-40217-007 @ In a shared listening activity, team up with a partner and be ready to listen to the speech at least twice. The webcode provides you with the link to Prince Harry's speech.

1. In a **first listening**, get a general understanding of Prince Harry's speech and the aspects he mentions. Jot down some notes that you consider to be relevant information.

Tips on vocab

mentoring the act of supporting and advising sb. with less experience to help them develop ■ **to percolate** to spread slowly ■ **quintessential** (*fml.*) being the most typical example or most important part of sth. ■ **to be struck** here: to be deeply impressed – **impactful** having a powerful effect on sb./sth. ■ **to mimic** to copy the way sb. speaks, move or behaves ■ **measure** (*fml.*) here: equal ■ **to acknowledge** to accept, admit or recognize sth. ■ **internal state** the condition inside a person's mind ■ **inspirational** filling you with hope or encouragement ■ **aligned** here: being together and connected ■ **North Star** here: sb. who guides you and leads you though life ■ **to collaborate** to work together with sb. ■ **alchemy** (*lit.*) a process that is so effective that it seems like magic ■ **to occur** to happen ■ **in sync** (*infml.*) reaching the same or related stage at the same time; to understand each other very well ■ **mutually** *gegenseitig* ■ **to pledge a commitment** *sich einer Verpflichtung verschreiben* ■ **to unlock** to make sth. more active and productive ■ **conscious** *bewusst* ■ **to inspire** to fill sb. with confidence and a desire to do sth. ■ **mentee** a person who is helped and guided by a mentor

2. Exchange your notes with your partner and briefly summarize **the gist** of the speech to each other.

3. **Listen** to Prince Harry's remarks **a second time**, now paying attention to **details** and taking notes on the aspects listed in the box below.
   - the impact of a role model
   - Harry's role as a father
   - leading by example
   - Harry's mother, Princess Diana
   - the need of mentors and mentoring
   → Prep Course *kompakt*, Listening Comprehension, p. 4

 Additionally, you can use worksheet 7.1 for a detailed listening comprehension.

ANALYSIS >>>>>>>

4. **Examine and analyse the relevant rhetorical devices* Prince Harry employed in his speech and explain how they serve to appeal to the audience and call them for action.**

Step 1:

Despite the fact that Prince Harry delivers his speech to honour the work of the young people present, his speech is clearly argumentative and aims at conveying his beliefs and convictions and influencing the listeners. Therefore, it is important to have a look at the **train of thought*** and **line of argument*** to better understand the structure and strategy of his speech. Following the topical order of the speech, filter out essential aspects and arrange them in a flow chart that illustrates the logical order of the arguments.

Example:

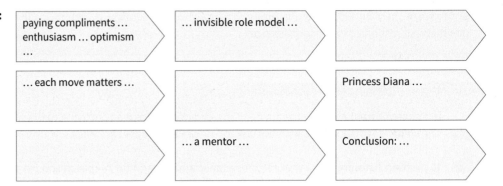

Step 2:

Now, focus on the most relevant rhetorical devices* in the speech as well as their function and effect. Use worksheet 7.2 for your respective notes.

→ Prep Course *kompakt*, Analysis of a Political Speech, p. 26
→ Prep Course *kompakt*, Analysis of a Non-Fictional Text, p. 22

Tip: Do not get lost in all the possible devices you could refer to but focus on the most relevant rhetorical devices* the speaker uses to convey his **message** and **appeal** to the audience. Think about what *you* would tell people if you want to motivate them, e. g. telling them
   - how great they are,
   - how successful they have already been,
   - about positive examples,
   - about your personal experience,
   - that you need their help (calling them to action).

Step 3:

If necessary, listen to the speech another time, then complete your notes in the grid and remember to add evidence from the speech and to identify the function and effect of the respective devices.

Tip: Of course, the predominant intention of most speeches is to influence and appeal to the audience. However, you are required to be more precise and go into detail in order to explain the function of certain elements and aspects of the speech at hand.

Tips on vocab ⟫⟫

- The speaker gives an overview of …
- The parts of the speech can be subdivided into thematic units …
- The choice of words gives the speech the character …
- The phrase/choice of words suggests …
- The speaker establishes a relationship between …
- She supports her view with …
- His formulations imply …

Tips on vocab ⟫⟫

The speaker …
- … enlarges on the situation of …
- … emphasizes/praises the progress made …
- … honours … for …
- … appeals to the listeners' understanding …
- … wants the audience to adapt his view on …
- … aims to get the listeners to act/to take action …
- … uses techniques of persuasion …
- … appeals in an emotional way …
- … alludes to his mother …
- … uses emotive language, like …
- … frequently uses …
- … uses stereotypes …
- … intends to …/… has the intention of …

Step 4:

Finally, using your results from the flow chart and the grid, write an analysis of the speech of about 350 words. Use the Tips on vocab boxes above for further help.

Tip: Make sure to paraphrase the speaker's remarks, using indirect speech.
Remember to
a) use the simple present mainly for your analysis and
b) give precise evidence from the speech to support the accuracy of your analysis.

Example:

On 2 July 2019, Prince Harry, the Duke of Sussex, delivered an honorary speech at the Diana Award National Youth Mentoring Summit, in which he emphasized the power of …
Prince Harry expresses his gratitude to …. He then continues to describe …, referring to …

@ **5.** In the middle part of his speech, Prince Harry refers to his mother, Princess Diana, and that she had an enormous impact on so many people.
Do research on Princess Diana and find out about
- her involvement in charity projects,
- her international work and support of victims of war and people suffering from deadly diseases,
- people's reaction to Diana's work.

 Give a 5-minute presentation of your findings in class.
→ Prep Course *kompakt*, Presentations, p. 44

ACTIVITIES

6. Team up with a partner and work on the cartoons below. First, describe the cartoons to each other and explain how they deal with the importance of role models.
Then, relate the cartoons to Prince Harry's understanding of a role model – what similarities and differences can you detect?
→ Prep Course *kompakt*, Analysis of Visuals, p. 30

"I want to be a role model."

GRAMMAR / LANGUAGE

7. Your school has a Chinese partner school and you are doing an e-twinning project. Your Chinese e-twinning partner is not really fluent in English and has difficulties in understanding the details of Prince Harry's speech. However, he or she is very interested in the empowerment of youth, and wants to know more about Prince Harry's speech.
Write your friend an e-mail in which you focus on essential parts of the speech. Use **indirect speech** to transmit Prince Harry's formulations as precisely as possible. Remember to **backshift tenses** where necessary.

Tip: Think about appropriate introductory verbs, phrases and sentences and do not overuse the verbs "say" and "think".

Tips on vocab »»»

Prince Harry …
described ■ gave a vivid illustration of ■ explained ■ pointed out ■ uttered ■ emphasized ■ praised ■ highlighted ■ honoured ■ referred to ■ remarked ■ applied to

Examples:
- Prince Harry emphasized that it was a pleasure to be there that afternoon …
- The Duke of Sussex highlighted that he could feel the inspiration that was marked by …
→ Appendix, Indirect Speech, p. 122
→ Appendix, Tenses, p. 130

Osval

Migrant Youth

In 2017, there were about 258 million migrants worldwide, of whom approximately 30 million were children and young people. The word migrant derives from the Latin verb 'migrare' which in fact has various meanings: to wander/to hike, to emigrate, to travel, to walk, etc. and generally refers to a person who moves from one place to another.

Do further research and try to find more precise definitions of the word 'migrant' and what groups of people it includes.

Migrant Youth by Osval,
15 April 2019

Tips on vocab ⟫⟫

a bagpacker ▪ to carry a bag-pack/rucksack ▪ to wear a (blue) T-shirt/blue jeans ▪ walking shoes/hiking boots ▪ (to sit on) a rolly bag/ wheeled cart ▪ to juggle with sth. ▪ globe(s) ▪ a white halo ▪ a light grey back-ground ▪ to have an emotion-less facial expression

The cartoon "Migrant Youth":

1. Describe the cartoon and, in a **first more general description**, focus on
   a) the most relevant eye-catching components,
   b) the use of colour, or the lack of it,
   c) visual symbols,
   d) your overall impression of the cartoon and the view it takes on migrants youth and travelling.

2. In the following, pay attention to **details** and describe the **different elements** of the cartoon:
- the arrangement of the different elements
- the combination of visual and textual elements (e. g. the title)
- allusions or references to political, social, economic or historical events

Tip: In order to avoid confusion or repetition, your description should follow a certain pattern, for example:
- Begin by describing the **foreground** of the cartoon.
- Continue by describing the people and objects in the **centre**.
- Complete your description by describing the **background** of the cartoon.
- → Prep Course *kompakt*, Analysis of Visuals, p. 30

3. Using your notes and the Tips on vocab box, describe the cartoon in a coherent text of about 150 – 200 words.

Tip: Use the present progressive as the general tense to describe the cartoons.

The article "Addressing Rural Youth Distress Migration":

4. Give an outline of the article (pp. 55) and state what it depicts about:
- the causes of migration
- the positive and negative impacts of migration on the areas of origin
- the problems rural areas have to face
- different kinds of migrants
- the development of global migration

Write a coherent text of about 150 words.

5. Analyse the cartoon and its message and explain the deeper meaning of the cartoon's title "Migrant Youth".

Step 1:
Examine the cartoon's predominant visual symbols, using your findings from assignments 1 and 2 and complete the grid below.

elements/components	function	message
visual elements ● young man/student ● bagpack ● …	→ …	→ young people taking opportunities
allusions/references ● going global ● …	→ …	→ …

Commonly, a cartoon aims at criticizing a situation or person or wants to make people aware of a problem in a humorous way. Often, there is a discrepancy or contradiction between the association it evokes and what people think or hope to see and reality.

In this case, the cartoonist plays with people's general understanding of the expression 'migrant youth'.

Step 2:

Examine the contradiction/discrepancy between

a) the image presented in the cartoon and what it implies, and

b) the cartoon's title 'Migrant Youth' and its implied meanings and people's associations.

SNG-40217-008 @
Worksheet 8.1

You can use worksheet 8.1 for your ideas and notes.

Step 3:

Examine the bar chart and explain the development of international migration.

→ Prep Course *kompakt*, Analysis of Statistical Data, p. 28

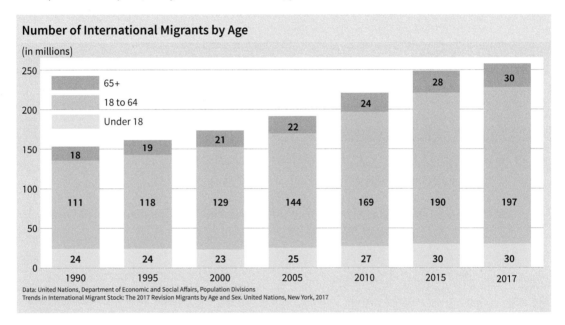

Number of International Migrants by Age

(in millions)

Legend:
- 65+
- 18 to 64
- Under 18

	1990	1995	2000	2005	2010	2015	2017
65+	18	19	21	22	24	28	30
18 to 64	111	118	129	144	169	190	197
Under 18	24	24	23	25	27	30	30

Data: United Nations, Department of Economic and Social Affairs, Population Divisions
Trends in International Migrant Stock: The 2017 Revision Migrants by Age and Sex. United Nations, New York, 2017

Step 4:

Finally, complete your analysis, adding your findings from step 3. Write an analysis of about 250 – 300 words, using the language help given in the Tips on vocab box below to connect your previous findings.

Tips on vocab ⟫⟫

to compare sth. with/to … ■ to make/draw a comparison between … and … ■ to relate sth. to/with … ■ to establish a connection between … and … ■ to connect … to/with … ■ to contrast with … ■ to draw a distinction between … ■ to have a literary (*wörtlich*) and a figurative (*übertragen*) meaning

6. Some people think that travelling, especially at a young age, broadens people's horizons and makes them more sensitive to global problems. Others, however, believe that 'travelling the world', especially in times of environmental and humanitarian crises is very foolish and a wasteful use of resources. Write an essay for your school magazine in which you assess the possible positive and negative aspects.

Tips: Before writing your essay, make a grid in which you juxtapose the pros and cons.

Example:

pro 🙂	con 🙁
● studying abroad helps to … ● a Work & Travel year can … ● …	● gap years are the luxury of people from rich nations … ● travelling to developing countries is … ● the environmental impact …

Tip: In your essay, follow the 'introduction – main part – conclusion' pattern to structure your text. Remember to use connectives/linkers to add to the fluency of your essay.

Tips on vocab >>>>

> on the one hand … on the other (hand) ■ on the contrary ■ by contrast ■ although ■ in spite of/despite ■ instead of ■ except for ■ alternatively ■ but

SNG-40217-008 @ Worksheet 8.2 **7.** Complete the table provided on worksheet 8.2 and collect vocabulary in connection with the topic of migration. Note: sometimes not all three columns can be filled in.

8. Find as many **synonyms** as possible for the words below, using your dictionary if necessary.

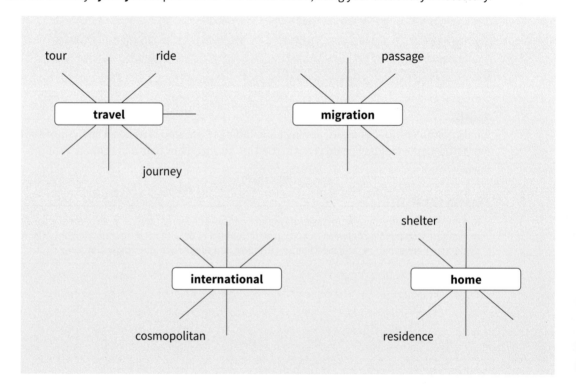

UNICEF

Addressing Rural Youth Distress[1] Migration

Migration out of rural areas is a complex issue, especially when caused by distress and lack of alternatives. The decision to migrate depends on a number of variables, including poverty, food insecurity, lack of employ-
5 ment opportunities, conflicts, natural disasters, poverty employment opportunities, and as well as household and individual characteristics. The impact of rural out-migration on the areas of origin can be positive or negative, or a combination of both: migrants and returnees
10 can contribute[2] investments, remittances[3] and skills for rural development, but distress migration can also result in the loss of the most vital[4] and dynamic part of the workforce, with negative consequences on agricultural[5] productivity. For this reason, policies and actions ad-
15 dressing distress migration need to both target its root causes[6] and minimize negative consequences, while at the same time enhance[7] the positive contribution of migration to rural areas. [...]

In 2017, there were 258 million people worldwide living
20 outside their country of birth; 30 million of them were children. Among the world's migrants are nearly 20 million refugees – some 10 million of whom are children – who have been forcibly[8] displaced[9] from their own countries. An additional 40 million people in 2017 were internally displaced due to conflict and violence, 25 and an estimated 17 million of those were children.

Overview

Since 1990, the proportion of international child migrants as part of the world's child population has remained remarkably stable at just over 1 per cent, but a 30 rising global population means that the absolute number of child migrants has increased in the past 27 years. The same is true for the overall international migrant population, which has remained at around 3 per cent of the total population. In 2017, there were 258 million in- 35 ternational migrants, compared to 153 million just 27 years before.

In 2017, the number of international migrants reached 258 million; 30 million of them were children. [...]

Note: International migrants refers to people living in a 40 country or area other than their country of birth.

https://data.unicef.org/topic/child-migration-and-displacement/
migration, December 2018 [24.07.2019]

---

[1] **distress** a feeling of extreme worry, sadness or pain – [2] **to contribute** *zu etw. beitragen* – [3] **remittance** an amount of money that you send to sb. – [4] **vital** ['vaɪtl] necessary or essential – [5] **agricultural** *landwirtschaftlich* – [6] **root cause** origin – [7] **to enhance** to improve the quality, amount or strength of sth. – [8] **forcibly** *mit/unter Zwang* – [9] **to displace** to force sb. out of his or her place of origin; *vertreiben*

Imagery consists of descriptive language that produces images (pictures), evokes associations in the reader's mind and adds symbolism. It includes figurative (*bildlich*) and metaphorical language and appeals to the five senses – taste, touch, sight, smell and sound. **Visual/graphic symbols** are used to represent forms, which allows for an interpretation beyond the literal (*wörtlich*) definition. Often, they illustrate unspoken feelings. There are simple graphic symbols (e.g. traffic signs, emojis) and more complex ones (e. g. butterfly → metamorphosis; owl → wisdom, etc.).

Jennifer Clement
Gun Love

My mother was a cup of sugar. You could borrow[1] her anytime.

My mother was so sweet, her hands were always birthday-party sticky[2]. Her breath held the five flavors of Life
5 Savers[3] candy.

And she knew all the love songs that are a university[4] for love. She knew "Slowly Walk Close to Me," Where Did You Sleep Last Night?," "Born Under A Bad Sign," and all the I'll-kill-you-if-you-leave-me songs.

10 But sweetness is always looking for Mr. Bad and Mr. Bad can pick out Miss Sweet in any crowd.

My mother opened her mouth in a great wide O and breathed him right into her body.

I couldn't understand. She knew all the songs, so why
15 would she get messed and stirred up with this man?

When he said his name was Eli she was down on her knees. [...]

My mother named me Pearl because, she said, You were so white. You came from a place that is far away from
20 any normal birthplace like a hospital or clinic.

She said, Nobody knew, and I gave you your birthday, to you all alone, by myself, in silence. I did not cry and you did not cry. [...]

She said, You were so small. You fit inside a hand towel. You were so white. More like a pearl than skin. You were 25 like ice or cloud, like a meringue[5]. I could almost see inside your body. I looked at your pale-blue stone eyes and named you. Just that, she said.

I was a pearl. People stared at me. I didn't know a different life. I didn't know what it was like to walk around 30 and not be noticed. They could think I was beautiful or ugly but, no matter what, everyone stared. Hands were always reaching out to touch my silver hair or the white glaze[6] of my cheek.

You're all luster[7], my mother said. Being with you is like 35 wearing pretty earrings and a new dress.

My mother lived in her father's house for two months after my birth without anyone knowing I was there.

She said, When I had to go to school or leave to do something, I placed you in the closet[8] in my room, all in the 40 dark, all wrapped up[9]. I made a bed for you on the shoe rack[10] with towels and my sweaters. I nested you there like a kitten. I used paper towels from the kitchen as diapers[11]. The house was so big, no one ever heard you cry.

You were born in a fairy tale, my mother said. 45

from *Gun Love* by Jennifer Clement. Hogarth Press, London, 2018, pp. 5 ff.

---

1. You have already read and dealt with another excerpt from the novel *Gun Love* in Skill 5.
   a) Read the excerpt from the novel.
   b) Some of the imagery employed in the text has already been highlighted.
   c) Use the checklist on the opposite page and first, determine the respective device; second, explain its function and effect.
   d) Detect and explain further imagery in the excerpt.

2. Using the criteria given in the checklist about visual and graphic symbols, work with the two visuals on the opposite page:
   a) How do they appeal to the reader's emotion?
   b) What is the message the cartoonist/photographer wants to convey?

---

[1] **to borrow** *etw. ausleihen* – [2] **sticky** *klebrig* – [3] **Life Savers** American ring-shaped candy – [4] **university** here: a source of information (about love) – [5] **meringue** [məˈræŋ] *Baiser, Schaumgebäck* – [6] **glaze** here: shiny softness – [7] **luster** brightness – [8] **closet** a small cupboard or room used to store things – [9] **to wrap sth. up** *einwickeln* – [10] **shoe rack** *Schuhregal* – [11] **diaper** [ˈdaɪəpə(r)] *Babywindel*

Banksy street art, *Slave Labour*, London 2010

A homeless mother and her children in Paris, France

Tips on vocab »»

1 a boy at pre-school age ■ to squat/to crouch (*hocken*) ■ sewing machine [ˈsəʊɪŋ məˌʃiːn] ■ old-fashioned ■ to have a distressed (*bekümmert*) facial expression ■ to sew [səʊ] sth. ■ bunting [*Wimpelgirlande*] ■ Union Jack/British national flag ■ dungarees (*Latzhose*)

2 to be huddled up ■ to sit on sb.'s lap ■ to huddle together (*zusammenkauern*) ■ huge plastic bags ■ one's belongings (*die Habe*) ■ to live from hand to mouth ■ to sit on a (dirty) pavement

3. This unit's title is "Growing Up – Being No Longer a Child!"
   Collect photographs, cartoons, graffiti and snippets from newspapers/magazines that reflect
   a) the implications of this headline.
   b) the various aspects that come to your mind when thinking abut 'growing up'.
    Present/display your wallpapers in class and discuss their implied messages.

Checklist

imagery	meaning/function/effect
metaphor	→ poetic comparison without 'like' or 'as#
simile	→ comparison using 'like' or 'as'
personification	→ objects/ideas/animals are given human characteristics (a smiling moon)
onomatopoeia	→ words that imitate a sound associated with a thing that is named (e. g. hum, cuckoo)
visual/graphic symbols	**meaning/function/effect**
items in focus/ visually dominant elements	→ guiding the viewer → eye-catcher
reduction to essentials/ simplification	→ focusing on the problem
snapshot character	→ emotional appeal to the viewer
colour(s)/lack of colour	→ focus on contrast → emotional appeal
caption	→ eyecatcher, evoking interest and curiosity

Putting You in the Picture – (Social) Media & You

Patrick Chappatte, 15 April 2018, in: Neue Zürcher Zeitung

Tips on vocab ⟫⟫⟫

to hug sb./each other ▪ to give sb. a hug ▪ to be friends with sb./each other ▪ a young man imperson-ating the Facebook company ▪ resemblance to Mark Zuckerberg ▪ to resemble Mark Zuckerberg, Face-book's owner ▪ to have similar features (*Gesichtszüge*) ▪ to wear a hoodie (with a Facebook logo) ▪ to steal sth. secretly from sb. ▪ pickpocketing (*Taschendiebstahl*) ▪ purse (*Portemonnaie*) ▪ to betray sb.'s trust/confidence

START-UP ACTIVITIES ⟫⟫⟫⟫⟫⟫

1. There are manifold social media and social networking services which customers worldwide can choose among.
   - Which personal media/networking service(s) do you use – and what made you choose this one/these ones?
   - Are you concerned that these companies might cheat you or abuse your data? Why (not)?
   - What makes you trust/mistrust a company in general?

   Discuss in class.

FACEBOOK'S 5 CORE VALUES

Be bold[1]

Building great things means taking risks. We have a saying: "The riskiest thing is to take no risks." In a world that's changing so quickty, you're guaranteed to fail if you don't take any risks. We encourage everyone to make bold decisions, even if that means being wrong some of the time.

Focus on impact[2]

To have the biggest impact, we need to focus on solving the most important problems. It sounds simple, but most companies do this poorly and waste a lot of time. We expect everyone at Facebook to be good at finding the biggest problems to work on.

Move fast

Moving fast enables us to build more things and learn faster. We're less afraid of making mistakes than we are of losing opportunities by moving too slowly. We are a culture of builders, the power is in your hands.

Be open

We believe that a more open world is a better world. The same goes for[3] our company. Informed people make better decisions and have a greater impact which is why we work hard to make sure everyone at Facebook has access[4] to as much information about the company as possible.

Build social value[5]

Facebook was created to make the world more open and connected, not just to build a company. We expect everyone at Facebook to focus every day on how to build real value for the worfd in everything they do.

https://www.facebook.com/media/set/?set=a.1655178611435493.1073741828.1633466236940064&type=3 [25.07.2019]

2. Briefly describe the cartoon, using the vocabulary given in the vocab box.

3. It has become common practice that a business or public organization draws up and publishes a 'mission statement' to express its aims and corporate philosophy to its customers and the public in general.
   a) Read Facebook's *5 Core Values* and extract the essential goals the company wants to achieve and wants its employees to realize.
   b) Looking from a potential Facebook user's/customer's perspective: are you satisfied with these values – or would you add further aspects, like transparency, honesty, etc.?

   c) Form groups and set up a mission statement for your ideal social networking company. Be careful to have the inward (= referring to the company and its employees) and the outward (= customers, users) perspective.

---

[1] **bold** not shy, and not frightened of danger – [2] **impact** a powerful effect that sth. has on a situation or another person – [3] **the same/that goes for sb./sth** *das Gleiche gilt für jdn./etw.* – [4] **access** ['ækses] *Zugang* – [5] **social value** a larger concept that includes a person's economic and subjective well-being and his or her ability to participate in making decisions

Max Schroth

Endstation Offline

a) Speculate about the meaning of the term "FOMO – The Fear of Missing Out". What kind of state does the word describe?

b) Describe the painting below. What does the way Steffen portrays himself reveal about his situation?

Self-portrait: While in therapy, Steffen painted himself. The portrait shows him sitting in front of his laptop. The red strokes represent the pain he suffered from sitting all day.

Tips on vocab >>>>

(to be at) the end of the line ■ a yellow halo ■ security ■ vicious circle ■ bent (*gebeugt*) ■ to bend (bent, bent) over sth. ■
backache ■ to have problems with your back ■ to have an aching behind (*Hintern*)

Tagelang verließ er die Wohnung nicht. Aß kaum, duschte unregelmäßig. Sogar den Gang zur Toilette schaffte er nur noch unter größten Anstrengungen[1]. Das alles erschien ihm unnötig. Steffen schaute sich im Netz eine
5 Serie nach der anderen an. Ob „Game of Thrones", „The Walking Dead" oder irgendwelche YouTube-Videos, er starrte pausenlos auf seinen Laptop. Bis zu 15 Stunden täglich. Steffen ist süchtig. Seine Droge: das Internet. Doch anders als Haschisch[2] oder Heroin[3] ist sein Stoff jederzeit in unbegrenzter Menge frei verfügbar[4].
Online-Süchtige nutzen das Internet so exzessiv[5], dass sie andere Lebensbereiche vernachlässigen. Freunde

10

[1] effort – [2] hash/cannabis – [3] heroin – [4] available – [5] excessive(ly)

und Familien werden ihnen gleichgültig. Sie schwänzen[6] die Schule. Pinkeln in Flaschen, um sich nicht vom Bildschirm entfernen zu müssen. Bei Entzug werden sie aggressiv. Nur eine neue Dosis kann sie beruhigen. Die Symptome ähneln denen eines Drogenabhängigen oder Alkoholkranken.

Nach Schätzungen von Experten sind in Deutschland über 700 000 Menschen von Online-Sucht betroffen. Zweieinhalb Millionen gelten als problematische Internetnutzer. Und mit voranschreitender[7] Digitalisierung werden es immer mehr: 99 Prozent der jungen Menschen in Deutschland sind online, 27 Prozent sagen sogar, dass sie praktisch nie offline sind. Dessen ist sich Bert te Wildt, Chefarzt[8] an der Psychosomatischen[9] Klinik Kloster Dießen, sicher. Junge Menschen seien besonders gefährdet. „In dieser Gruppe geht man von drei bis vier Prozent aus, was als Indiz[10] dafür zu werten[11] ist, dass die Zahlen weiter steigen werden."

Fast jeder Mensch besitzt ein Smartphone und ist so rund um die Uhr online. Doch für Chefarzt te Wildt ist die Internet-Nutzungsdauer[12] lediglich ein Richtwert und nicht maßgeblich[13] für eine Diagnose. „Wer beispielsweise beruflich viel online ist, ist nicht gleich auch süchtig", erklärt der 49-Jährige.

Die Verführung, der sich vor allem junge Menschen immer häufiger nicht entziehen können, entsteht eher in der Freizeit[14]. Die Sehnsucht[15], 24/7 am Leben einer virtuellen Gemeinschaft teilnehmen zu wollen, bloß nichts zu verpassen. Der Psychologe[16] Dan Ariely von der renommierten[17] Duke University nannte diese Sorge „Fear of Missing Out" (kurz: FOMO). Und im Zeitalter der ständig verfügbaren[18] sozialen Medien eskaliert[19] diese Angst. Es gehört eine gewisse Routine dazu, bis wir realisieren, dass Facebook-Fotos von Mittagsmahl oder Alpenglühen[20] kein Erlebnis reproduzieren, sondern synthetische Gefühle darstellen. Wer es mit der Achtsamkeit[21] und also auch mit sich selbst ernst nimmt, gönnt sich digitale Auszeiten. So wird aus FOMO die JOMO: „Joy of Missing Out". Die Freude an der Ruhe. [...]

Steffen ist von schmächtiger[22] Statur. Er hat kurze braune Haare und einen Dreitagebart[23]. In seinem blau-weißen Karohemd sitzt er am Tisch im Konferenzsaal. Er nippt an seinem Kaffee und hält kurz inne. Dann beginnt er seinen Weg in die Sucht zu erzählen: „Angefangen hat alles im Grundschulalter." Er wuchs in schwierigen Familienverhältnissen auf, war zu Hause oft allein. Beide Elternteile arbeiteten viel und hatten für ihren Sohn keine Zeit. Es kam oft zu Streit. Er fühlte sich einsam.

Aus Langeweile verbrachte er viel Zeit am Computer. „Das war damals zwar noch nicht pathologisch[24] oder problematisch, aber ich hatte schon relativ früh einen Zugang dazu und habe das auch viel zur Stressregulation verwendet." In der digitalen Welt fand er endlich die Geborgenheit[25], nach der er zu Hause vergeblich gesucht hat. Sie wurde sein Ruhepol[26]. „Ich konnte mich da einfach reinbeamen und musste dann nicht mehr meine Umgebung[27] wahrnehmen oder an Probleme denken, die ich irgendwie nicht lösen konnte." [...]

Im schlimmsten Fall kann die Online-Sucht sogar tödlich sein. Menschen, die sich ums Leben zocken[28], sind mittlerweile keine Seltenheit mehr. Te Wildt verweist auf einen besonders tragischen Fall in einem taiwanischen Internet-Café aus dem Jahr 2015. Ein 32-jähriger Mann starb nach einem dreitägigen Computerspiel-Marathon an Herzversagen[29]. Sein Ableben wurde zunächst noch nicht einmal bemerkt. Die anderen Computerspieler wähnten ihn schlafend. „Bei ihm hatte bereits die Leichenstarre[30] eingesetzt, als die Rettungskräfte[31] eintrafen." [...]

Für Steffen hat die Sucht zwar noch keine lebensbedrohlichen Ausmaße angenommen. Allerdings spürt er erste Anzeichen dafür, dass Komaglotzen[32] ihn physisch krank[33] macht. [...]

In seinem Zimmer kann Steffen sich entspannen. Überall liegen Bücher, Zeitungen und selbst gemalte Bilder herum. Er hat diese Beschäftigungsmöglichkeiten[34] neu für sich entdeckt. Es gibt aber auch kaum Alternativen. Das einzige technische Gerät, auf das er Zugriff hat, ist ein kleines Radio. Sein Handy hat er nach drei Wochen abgegeben. „Das hat mir am Anfang als Methadon[35] genützt." Für ihn ein erster Sieg.

FOCUS, 18/2019, 27 April 2019, pp. 70 ff.

---

[6] to play truant – [7] to progress – [8] chief physician – [9] psychosomatic – [10] indicator – [11] to assess sth. as – [12] period of use – [13] irrelevant – [14] leisure time – [15] desire – [16] psychologist – [17] renowned – [18] available – [19] to escalate – [20] alpenglow – [21] mindfulness – [22] wispy – [23] three-day beard – [24] pathological – [25] feeling of security – [26] haven of tranquility – [27] surroundings/environment – [28] to gamble – [29] cardiac arrest – [30] rigor mortis – [31] paramedics – [32] binge watching – [33] mentally ill – [34] offer of (various) activities – [35] methadone

M 1. **Against the background of a growing number of internet-addicted people, you have done some research and found an international online forum that discusses the issue and offers help. They are always looking for further information and institutions or people that offer (professional) help. Mediate the German magazine article at hand and write an e-mail to the editors of the forum that contains the most relevant information.**

Tip: Although you are given quite a number of annotations, be careful <u>not</u> to translate the magazine article word for word. Use the annotations to get **a general idea** of how to **mediate** and **contextualize** the article with regard to the content.

Step 1:
Read the article and look out for relevant information and keywords on these topics:
- Steffen's life before the therapy
- online addiction – facts and data
- dangers for young people
- turning FOMO into JOMO
- Steffen's therapy
- an example from Taiwan

Step 2:

M Now sort your findings and mediate them into English. Fill in the respective English words, phrases and expressions and complete the grid below.

Steffen's life before the therapy	online addiction – facts and data	dangers for young people
● Watching video clips 15 hours a day ● …	● 700 000 people … ● …	● …
turning FOMO into JOMO	**Steffen's therapy**	**an example from Taiwan**
● 24/7 … ● …	● …	● …

Tip: You can use the annotations and the dictionary for specific technical terms – but try to formulate and paraphrase difficult expressions and passages in your own words as much as possible. The Info box below will give you additional help.
→ Prep Course *kompakt*, Mediation, p. 36

Info ⟫⟫

Paraphrasing means rewriting somebody else's thoughts or formulations in your own words. This often requires you to
- use simpler language and less complex sentences and formulations.
- transform technical terms into everyday language.
- convey a message to non-experts.
- use synonyms of certain ideas or concepts.
- refer to examples to illustrate a complicated or complex matter.

Step 3:
Subdivide the article into thematic units and find a suitable headline for each paragraph, using your own words.

Step 4:

Remember, you are asked to mediate the magazine article to an international online forum. You want to inform them about the examples and information given in the article at hand.

Tip: First, reactivate your knowledge of how to write a formal e-mail:
- Focus on the relevant information given in the article.
- Avoid wordy explanations.
- Structure your e-mail in visual as well as thematic paragraphs to give it more clarity.

Step 5:

Using your notes and answers, write an e-mail about online addiction and Steffen's situation, mediating the German magazine article into a coherent text of about 250 – 300 words.

Tip: Begin your e-mail with a few introductory words and remember to include the source where you found the information (i. e. name of the magazine, name of the author, title of the article, publication date, etc.).

Example:

Dear …,
Only recently I found a most interesting magazine article about how to treat the internet addiction of young people. The article, entitled …, was published in the German … on …

ANALYSIS

2. Examine how the German magazine article reports on the matter and pay attention to specific formulations and their effect and message.

Examples:
- „Tagelang verließ er … Aß kaum … den Gang zur Toilette …"
  → emotional impact; human interest; disgust and pity are evoked in the reader
- „Aß kaum, duschte unregelmäßig … Bis zu 15 Stunden täglich …"
  → short, elliptical* sentences, paratactic*; easy to understand
- „Fast jeder Mensch … rund um die Uhr …"
  → generalization; (indirect) appeal to the reader

ACTIVITIES

3. Being an online and digital device user yourself, take the opportunity to respond to the information and warnings given in the article. Write a letter to the editor in which you
a) state your opinion on the topic,
b) respond to specific statements made in the article, commenting on and/or evaluating them from your point of view,
c) suggest possible alternatives or solutions.
→ Prep Course *kompakt*, Writing a Letter to the Editor, p. 56

4. Compare the article at hand to the online article by Elizabeth Hartney which is provided on worksheet 9.1.
- What further details on internet addiction and its impact does the article provide?
- Who do you think are the potential addressees of these articles? Discuss in class.
→ Prep Course *kompakt*, Conversation and Discussion, p. 38

GRAMMAR / LANGUAGE ⟩⟩⟩⟩⟩⟩

SNG-40217-009
Worksheet 9.1 **5.** Read the online article about internet addiction provided on worksheet 9.1.
Think about whether to use the **adjective or adverb** and cross out the incorrect alternative.
→ Appendix, Adjectives and Adverbs, p. 115

M **6.** Mediate the sentences below, which are taken from the omitted parts of the magazine article, into English.
Use the **passive voice** whenever possible to make your formulations less personal.
→ Appendix, Passive, p. 128

- In seinem Buch „Digital Junkies" warnt te Wildt vor der Suchtgefahr durch das World Wide Web.
- Viele Videospiele generieren durch das Zufallsprinzip Erfolge und stimulieren das Belohnungssystem im Gehirn.
- Die Weltgesundheitsorganisation (WHO) plant Internetsucht als „Gaming Disorder" in ihren Krankheitskatalog aufzunehmen.
- Bisher tragen die Krankenkassen Kosten von 250 Euro pro Tag.
- Die Sucht zerstört soziale Kompetenzen und macht Menschen unsicher.

7. Imagine Steffen writes a diary and asks himself what would have happened if he had not …
Write that diary entry, using **conditional III** sentences and reflect on what would or could have been different.

Examples:
- If I hadn't been alone that often, I wouldn't have felt lonely.
- If I had begun the therapy earlier, I could have …
→ Appendix, Conditional Sentences (If-Clauses), p. 119

Faktenreport: Internet-Sucht

AWARENESS ▶≫≫

Step 1: In a Think! Pair! Share!-activity, reflect on and discuss the quotations from Mark Zuckerberg below. Bear in mind that Facebook's 2018 revenue (*Einnahmen*) was US$55.838 billion, with about 2.3 billion monthly active users.

> **1** Think about what people are doing on Facebook today. They're keeping up with their friends and family, but they're also building an image and identity for themselves, which in a sense is their brand. They're connecting with the audience that they want to connect to. It's almost a disadvantage if you're not on it now.
>
> **2** Facebook was not originally created to be a company. It was built to accomplish a social mission – to make the world more open and connected.
>
> **3** The question isn't 'What do we want to know about people?', it's 'What do people want to tell about themselves?'

Step 2: Divide the class into two groups, with one group looking at one of the cartoons below.
a) Describe the cartoons, paying attention to all the details. Use the language help given in the Tips on vocab boxes.
b) Find out and explain what the cartoons poke fun at (*verspotten*) and criticize about social media in general and Facebook in particular.
→ Prep Course *kompakt*, Analysis of Visuals, p. 30

Silvano Mello, 12 October 2016

Tips on vocab ≫≫

to sit with one's legs spread out ■ to bend over sth. ■ to look exhausted ■ to have a bleak (*niedergeschlagen, trostlos*) facial expression ■ to be chained up to an iron ball and chain ■ to have an inscription (Facebook company logo) ■ spiderweb

"Nice work – let's take a quick social-media break."

Trevor Spaulding, 16 May 2016, in: New Yorker

Tips on vocab ≫≫

at a gym ■ to do exercises ■ to do a workout ■ to do weightlifting ■ to sweat

COMPREHENSION ▶▶▶▶▶

M 👥 **1.** Team up with a partner and mediate the data presented in the different illustrations and graphics below using the Tips on vocab boxes.
→ Prep Course *kompakt*, Mediation, p. 36

SNG-40217-010
Worksheet 10.1 @ **2.** In order to check your overall understanding of the infographic do the tasks provided on worksheet 10.1.

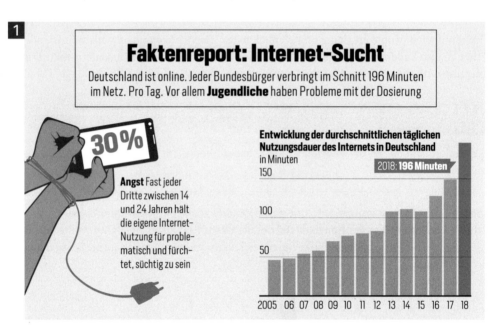

1

Faktenreport: Internet-Sucht

Deutschland ist online. Jeder Bundesbürger verbringt im Schnitt 196 Minuten im Netz. Pro Tag. Vor allem **Jugendliche** haben Probleme mit der Dosierung

30 %

Angst Fast jeder Dritte zwischen 14 und 24 Jahren hält die eigene Internet-Nutzung für problematisch und fürchtet, süchtig zu sein

Entwicklung der durchschnittlichen täglichen Nutzungsdauer des Internets in Deutschland
in Minuten
150
2018: **196 Minuten**
100
50

2005 06 07 08 09 10 11 12 13 14 15 16 17 18

Tips on vocab ▶▶▶

> bar chart ▪ to rank first … second … last ▪ the highest/lowest figure ▪ no/a little/a big difference between ▪ the figures are similar to/different from ▪ to experience a sudden rise ▪ a striking/slow rise in

2 **Computerspiel-/Internet-bezogene Störungen** Angaben in Prozent
■ männlich ■ weiblich

Jugendliche sind besonders suchtgefährdet. Mädchen stärker als Jungen

7,1
4,5
2,8 **2,8**

12–17 Jahre   18–25 Jahre

Tips on vocab ▶▶▶

> bar chart ▪ in comparison with ▪ in contrast to ▪ a striking difference between ▪ comparable figures ▪ the age group of …

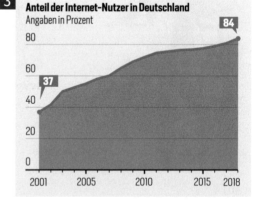

3 **Anteil der Internet-Nutzer in Deutschland**
Angaben in Prozent
80
84
60
37
40
20
0

2001   2005   2010   2015 2018

Tips on vocab ▶▶▶

> line graph ▪ to reach a peak to increase/rise/ go up ▪ a gradual/steady/continual line ▪ continually rising ▪ a significant rise

4

Häufigkeit der Internet-Nutzung Wofür sie das Internet täglich nutzen: Jugendliche 12–17 Jahre

Kommunikation	Unterhaltung	Information	Computerspiel

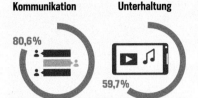

80,6%

59,7%

24,0%

24,0%

Viele Fallen Chatten, Musik hören, Videos schauen, Spiele zocken. Die digitale Welt lockt vor allem Jugendliche mit ihrem Entertainment-Angebot. Neun von zehn Teenies sind täglich online

> **Tips on vocab** ⧸⧸⧸
>
> pie chart ■ a share of
> … % ■ the circle stands
> for ■ percentagewise ■
> the chart reveals the per-
> centage of …

5

Viele Fallen Chatten, Musik hören, Videos schauen, Spiele zocken. Die digitale Welt lockt vor allem Jugendliche mit ihrem Entertainment-Angebot. Neun von zehn Teenies sind täglich online

Von der Gruppe der Abhängigen angegebene Hauptaktivität, Pinta-Studie 2013

36,6%	36,6%	26,8%
Online-Spiele	soziale Netzwerke	andere Internet-Anwendung

Suchtpotenzial Die meisten Betroffenen sind süchtig nach sozialen Medien oder Online-Spielen wie „World of Warcraft". Aber auch Pornos, Shoppen oder Filmeschauen können süchtig machen

> **Tips on vocab** ⧸⧸⧸
>
> a horizontal bar ■ to be
> divided into thirds ■
> the figures are (almost)
> identical ■ a similar num-
> ber of people ■ the figures
> show an identical number
> of users

FOCUS, 18/2019, 27 April 2019, p. 76

ANALYSIS ⧸⧸⧸⧸

3. Analyse the presented data on the extent and different forms of internet addiction in Germany and try to explain the correlated causes for this development as well as the possible consequences for the people.

Step 1:
Study **illustration no. 1** and explain the increase of time spent on the internet as well as the increase in the number of users in Germany.

Tip: In addition to the information given in the infographic, use further aspects given in the Info box to find possible causes for the depicted development.

Step 2:
Try to find reasons for the data given in **illustration no. 2**.

Step 3:
Explain the rise in the overall number of internet users depicted in **illustration no. 3**.

Step 4:
Explain the information given in **illustration no. 4**. What makes online
- chatting,
- entertainment,
- research,
- gaming

particularly interesting for 12–17-year-olds?

Step 5:

"World of Warcraft", porn movies, shopping, watching videos … What actually made internet users addicted? Try to find answers in **illustration no. 5** and the Info box.

Info ▶▶

The development and release of digital media and gadgets	
1993	portable MP3 players
1997	Google is registered
2000	USB flash drives
2001	Wikipedia
2003	Skype
2005	YouTube
2006	Facebook
2007	Dropbox – Apple TV – iPhone – mobile GPS – Netflix
2009	WhatsApp
2010	iPad – Instagram
2011	Facebook has 550 million users
2014	Google Glass – Amazon Alexa
2015	Apple Watch – Amazon Echo
2016	Tesla Powerwall – Amazon Echo Dot – Pokemon Go
2017	Surface laptop
2018	Google Pay

Step 6:

Finally, write a coherent analysis of the infographic and various data and explain the interdependencies and correlations.

Tip: Use this structure for your analysis:
- **introduction** (title, author, topic, time of publication)
- **main part**
  a) identifying and describing the data
  b) comparing the relevant data
  c) relating the data to other data/information available (→ contextualization)
  d) drawing conclusions and explaining the facts and data
- **conclusion** (summing up the main/most relevant aspects in one to two sentences)
→ Prep Course *kompakt*, Writing an Analysis, p. 48
→ Prep Course *kompakt*, Analysis of Statistical Data, p. 28

Example:

The infographic, published by the German magazine *Focus* on … presents and illustrates data on the state of … the five different sections of the infographic present … are focusing on …

4. Critically evaluate and comment on the infographic.
- To what extent are the statistics informative and differentiated?
- In what way does the presented data match your own experiences with the use of internet services?
→ Prep Course *kompakt*, Writing a Comment and a Review, p. 52

Present your results in class and discuss whether (or not) they match the view conveyed by the magazine *Focus*.
→ Prep Course *kompakt*, Conversation and Discussion, p. 38

GRAMMAR / LANGUAGE ⟩⟩⟩⟩⟩⟩

5. Compare the words and phrases from the box below and form **collocations** (= a combination of related words). Some words can be used more than once.

Example: to surf the net

> to go on • online shopping • a website • to access • the internet • social networks •
> ~~the net~~ • to use • to download sth. from • images • to maintain • to navigate • a file •
> to do • information • to browse • online • to delete • to attach • ~~to surf~~ • to display

SNG-40217-010
Worksheet 10.2 **6.** Find further **collocations** and do the tasks on worksheet 10.2.

Disconnect to Reconnect

eMail: support@endnowfoundation.org | www.endnowfoundation.org |

Save your life from getting drowned in the world of mobiles.

Join ENNOW! And help yourself and your well-wishers from turning victims of Digital Abuse by putting an end to it.

Advocacy on Combating Cyber Crime, Cyberbullying, Smartphone Addiction Fake News, Online Surveillance and other Digital Abuse

Stand up and speak up for a change.

| eMail: support@endnowfoundation.org | www.endnowfoundation.org |

Before your mobile takes control of your life, break-free.

Join ENNOW! And help yourself and your well-wishers from turning victims of Digital Abuse by putting an end to it.

Advocacy on Combating Cyber Crime, Cyberbullying, Smartphone Addiction Fake News, Online Surveillance and other Digital Abuse

Stand up and speak up for a change.

| eMail: support@endnowfoundation.org | www.endnowfoundation.org |

Selfie - Awareness

Be Aware of whats behind you.

Join ENNOW! And help yourself and your well-wishers from turning victims of Digital Abuse by putting an end to it.

Advocacy on Combating Cyber Crime, Cyberbullying, Smartphone Addiction Fake News, Online Surveillance and other Digital Abuse

Stand up and speak up for a change.

| eMail: support@endnowfoundation.org | www.endnowfoundation.org |

"End Now Foundation is India's first non-profit organization which aims at making the ever-evolving digital era transparent and free from Cyber Crime, Social Engineering Crimes, Smartphone/Internet Addiction, Cyber-Bullying. Online Surveillance and Online Hoax News and other digital abuse."

https://endnowfoundation.org [10.08.2019]

 1. Togehter with a partner, choose one of the campaign posters on the opposite page and describe it to each other, paying attention to details. Particularly focus on:
- the use of colour(s)
- the graphical presentation
- the combination of textual and visual elements
- the symbolic meaning of certain elements
- the overall impression
- the use of rhetorical devices, e. g. play on words/puns, key words, positive/negative emotive words
- the message of the respective poster

2. Use your experiences as a consumer of advertising and use advertising strategies to make (young) people aware of the potential risks and dangers of excessive internet use.

 Team up in a group of four students each and
a) compile a folder/brochure that is both informative and appealing to its readers,
b) design posters that inform about the problem,
c) plan and launch a campaign at your school that addresses students of different ages.

3. Additionally, and/or alternatively, compile short video clips ('commercials') that promote the careful and responsible use of the internet and social networks and give people advice on how to identify and deal with potential internet addiction.

Tip: Use the aspects listed in the check list for further help and ideas.

Checklist

elements ...	functions ...
Compilation and design of posters • banner headline/caption • visual eyecatcher • colour(s) • catchy slogans using – alliterations/onomatopoeia/neologisms/superlatives/proverbs/ comparatives/suggestive/rhetorical questions	→ attracting people's attention → evoking curiosity and emotion → delivering a message → appealing → eye-catching → influencing people and making them want to join the campaign
compilation of brochures • facts, data, factual information • well-chosen/appealing motives – visual symbols/icons/funny/shocking pictures/provocative photos	→ liability of the information → credibility of the authors → evoking interest and curiosity → appeal to take action

Living in a Material World?! – Consumption & Environment

Ed Hawkins
Warming Stripes

In May 2018, Ed Hawkins, a climate scientist and professor at the University of Reading, England, published a chronologically ordered series of coloured vertical stripes aimed at visualizing global warming.

> "I wanted to communicate temperature changes in a way that was simple and intuitive, removing all the distractions of standard climate graphics so that the long-term trends and variations in temperature are crystal clear. Our visual system will do the interpretation of the stripes without us even thinking about it."
>
> https://earther.gizmodo.com/this-climate-visualization-belongs-in-a-damn-museum-1826307536, 25 May 2018 [20.09.2019]

Annual global temperatures from 1850–2018 with each stripe representing one year. The colour scale represents the change in global temperatures covering 1.35°C.

Annual temperatures in Germany from 1881–2018 with each stripe representing one year. The colour scale goes from 6.6°C (dark blue) to 10.3°C (dark red).

Wir haben die Schnauze voll.

Hilf unseren Meeren mit deiner Spende:
wwf.de/plastikflut

STOPP DIE PLASTIK FLUT

Der WWF arbeitet weltweit mit Menschen, Unternehmen und Politik zusammen, um die Vermüllung der Meere zu stoppen.
Hilf mit deiner Spende! **WWF-Spendenkonto: IBAN DE06 5502 0500 0222 2222 22**

Tips on vocab »»»

a dolphin with its jaws wide open ▪ looking directly into the viewer's eye ▪ different kinds of plastic trash ▪ disposable packaging ▪ disposable plastic cups/bottles/plates/straws ▪ aluminium/tin/plastic foil ▪ to suffocate from sth. ▪ to digest sth. ▪ to get sth. into one's system ▪ WWF logo ▪ panda bear ▪ banner headline/caption ▪ to be fed up (to the back teeth) with sb./sth. (*infml.*) ▪ appeal to the viewer to stop the flood of plastic ▪ appeal to donate money ▪ to launch a campaign

START-UP ACTIVITIES »»»»»»»

1. Take a close look at the warming stripes and
   a) describe the (obvious) trends in temperature in Germany and globally,
   b) exchange your opinion of the graphics and what they represent and reveal.

@ **2.** Do further research on the matter and prepare short presentations. Here are some helpful websites:
   • https://en.wikipedia.org/wiki/warming_stripes
   • https://www.climate-lap-book.ac.uk/2018/warming-stripes

3. The third visual depicts another alarming global development: the thoughtless and irresponsible use and waste of plastic.
   Team up with a partner and
   a) describe the various visual and textual elements of the poster,
   b) explain the poster's symbolic meaning and intended message.
   → Prep Course *kompakt*, Analysis of Visuals, p. 30

George Monbiot

Too Right It's Black Friday[1]: Our Relentless[2] Consumption Is Trashing the Planet

AWARENESS >>>>>>>>>

Back in the day, people were used to sorting (*reparieren*) things, e. g. socks with holes or stockings with runs (*Laufmaschen*) were not thrown away but darned (*stopfen*) and mended.

Step 1:

Interview your parents or grandparents about which household items or textiles they (had) repaired and why they (or their parents) didn't throw them away.

Step 2:

 Team up with a partner and describe the cartoon below. What does it reveal or criticize about the 'throwaway mentality' of people today?

Step 3:

Discuss in class: What makes people today <u>not</u> repair most of the household items or textiles but buy new ones instead?

Tips on vocab >>>

then: a single-family house behind a wooden fence ■ to pass sth. over to sb. ■ an electric iron ■ a mechanic in a repair shop ■ to repair/to mend sth.

now: a hand/arm reaching out of the window ■ to dispose of sth./to throw sth. away ■ a heap of rubbish ■ household items ■ washing machine, refrigerator, electric iron, monitor ■ to board sth. up ■ spiderweb ■ to shut down a business

The Throw-Away Society by Popa Matumula, 17 May 2012

[1] **Black Friday** the Friday after Thanksgiving when stores in the US reduce the price of goods in order to attract customers who want to start their Christmas shopping – [2] **relentless** continuing in a severe and extreme way

1. While reading the text, finish the following statements using evidence and information from the text.
   a) (Economic) growth is …
   b) Rising consumption is destroying the planet because …
   c) Politics and marketing tell us that …
   d) People are ending their own options of survival by …
   e) Green consumption is a false promise because …
   f) Many people want to be 'green' and recycle but …
   g) The belief that economic growth is essential for humankind's survival is wrong because …
   h) Our current system is based on …
   i) A different system would include …

Growth must go on – it's the political imperative everywhere, and it's destroying the Earth. But there's no way of greening it, so we need a new system

5 Everyone wants everything – how is that going to work? The promise of economic growth is that the poor can live like the rich and the rich can live like the oligarchs[1]. But already we are bursting[2] through the physical limits of the planet that sustains[3] us. Climate break-
10 down, soil[4] loss, the collapse of habitats[5] and species, the sea of plastic, insectageddon[6]: all are driven by rising consumption. The promise of private luxury for everyone cannot be met: neither the physical nor the ecological space exists.

15 But growth must go on: this is everywhere the political imperative. And we must adjust our tastes accordingly. In the name of autonomy[7] and choice, marketing uses the latest findings in neuroscience[8] to break down our defences[9]. Those who seek to resist must, like the Sim-
20 ple Lifers in *Brave New World*[10], be silenced – in this case by the media. With every generation, the baseline of normalised consumption shifts. Thirty years ago, it was ridiculous to buy bottled water, where tap water[11] is clean and abundant[12]. Today, worldwide, we use a mil-
25 lion plastic bottles a minute.

Every Friday is a Black Friday, every Christmas a more garish[13] festival of destruction. Among the snow saunas, portable watermelon coolers and smartphones for dogs with which we are urged[14] to fill our lives, my #ex-
30 tremecivilisation prize now goes to the PancakeBot: a 3D batter[15] printer that allows you to eat the Mona Lisa, the Taj Mahal, or your dog's bottom every morning. In practice, it will clog up[16] your kitchen for a week until you decide you don't have room for it. For junk like this,
35 we're trashing the living planet, and our own prospects of survival. Everything must go.

The ancillary[17] promise is that, through green consumerism, we can reconcile[18] perpetual[19] growth with planetary survival. But a series of research papers reveal
40 that there is no significant difference between the ecological footprints of people who care and people who don't. One recent article, published in the journal Environment and Behaviour, finds that those who identify themselves as conscious consumers use more energy
45 and carbon than those who do not.

Why? Because environmental awareness tends to be higher among wealthy people. It is not attitudes that govern our impact on the planet but income. The richer we are, the bigger our footprint, regardless of our good
50 intentions. Those who see themselves as green consumers, the research found, "mainly focused on behaviours that had relatively small benefits".

I know people who recycle meticulously[20], save their plastic bags, carefully measure the water in their kettles,
55 then take their holidays in the Caribbean, cancelling any environmental savings a hundredfold[21]. I've come to believe that the recycling licences[22] their long-haul[23]

---

[1] **oligarch** one of a small group of powerful people who control a country or an industry – [2] **to burst** to break open suddenly – [3] **to sustain** to keep alive – [4] **soil** *Mutterboden* – [5] **habitat** the natural environment in which plants or animals usually live – [6] **insectageddon** neologism which means the mass extinction of insects – [7] **autonomy** [ɔːˈtɒnəmi] the right to be independent and govern oneself – [8] **neuroscience** [ˌnjʊərəʊˈsaɪəns] the scientific study of the nervous system and the brain – [9] **defence** protection against attack or infection – [10] **Simple Lifers in *Brave New World*** people designed in laboratories and living a careless life without worries and dangers; reference to Aldous Huxley's 1932 dystopian novel *Brave New World* – [11] **tap water** *Leitungswasser* – [12] **abundant** more than enough – [13] **garish** unpleasantly bright – [14] **to urge sb.** *jdn. drängen* – [15] **batter** *Teig* – [16] **to clog up** *vollstopfen* – [17] **ancillary** providing support or help – [18] **to reconcile** *in Übereinstimmung bringen* – [19] **perpetual** continuing for ever – [20] **meticulously** *akribisch* – [21] **a hundredfold** a hundred times as much – [22] **to licence sth.** *etw. erlauben, genehmigen* – [23] **long-haul** travelling a long distance

flights. It persuades people they've gone green, enabling them to overlook their greater impacts.

60 None of this means that we should not try to reduce our footprint, but we should be aware of the limits of the exercise. Our behaviour within the system cannot change the outcomes of the system. It is the system itself that needs to change. [...]

65 A global growth rate of 3% means that the size of the world economy doubles every 24 years. This is why environmental crises are accelerating[24] at such a rate. Yet the plan is to ensure that it doubles and doubles again, and keeps doubling in perpetuity[25]. In seeking to de-
70 fend the living world from the maelstrom[26] of destruction, we might believe we are fighting corporations and governments and the general foolishness of humankind. But they are all proxies[27] for the real issue: perpetual growth on a planet that is
75 not growing.

Those who justify this system insist that economic growth is essential for the relief of poverty. But a paper in the World Economic Re-
80 view finds that the poorest 60% of the world's people receive only 5% of the additional income generated by rising GDP[28]. As a result, $111 of growth is required for every $1 re-
85 duction in poverty. This is why, on current trends, it would take 200 years to ensure that everyone receives $5 a day. By this point, average[29] per capita income will have
90 reached $1m a year, and the economy will be 175 times bigger than it is today. This is not a formula for

poverty relief. It is a formula for the destruction of everything and everyone. [...]

95 Green consumerism, material decoupling[30], sustainable growth: all are illusions, designed to justify an economic model that is driving us to catastrophe[31]. The current system, based on private luxury and public squalor[32], will immiserate[33] us all: under this model, luxury and deprivation[34] are one beast with two heads.
100 We need a different system, rooted[35] not in economic abstractions but in physical realities, that establish the parameters[36] by which we judge its health. We need to build a world in which growth is unnecessary, a world of private sufficiency[37] and public luxury. And we must
105 do it before catastrophe forces our hand[38].

https://www.theguardian.com/commentisfree/2017/nov/22/black-friday-consumption-killing-planet-growth, 22 November 2017 [04.05.2019]

Jeff Koterba, 20 November 2018

SNG-40217-011 @
Worksheet 11.1

COMPREHENSION

2. After a second reading, subdivide the text into paragraphs, following the thematic units of the text. Find a suitable headline for each paragraph using your own words.

3. The article contains a lot of formal or idiomatic and specialized vocabulary that you might not know. In order to get a better understanding of the details do the exercise provided on worksheet 11.1.

---

[24] **to accelerate** to go faster – [25] **in perpetuity** (*fml.*) forever – [26] **maelstrom** *Sog* – [27] **proxy** *Stellvertreter* – [28] **GDP** (*abbr.*) Gross Domestic Product; the total value of goods and services produced in a country in one year – [29] **average** *durchschnittlich* – [30] **to decouple** *etw. entkoppeln* – [31] **catastrophe** [kəˈtæstrəfi] – [32] **squalor** *Elend* – [33] **to immiserate** (*fml.*) to make sth. miserable – [34] **deprivation** *Entbehrung, Mangel* – [35] **to root in sth.** *in etw. wurzeln* – [36] **parameter** *Faktor* – [37] **sufficiency** (*fml.*) *Hinlänglichkeit* – [38] **to force sb.'s hand** *jdm. zum Handeln zwingen*

⫸⫸⫸⫸⫸ **ANALYSIS** ⫸⫸⫸⫸⫸

4. Examine and analyse the author's stance on (green) consumption, taking into consideration
a) the line of argument,   b) the type of text,   c) relevant stylistic devices.
→ Prep Course *kompakt*, Analysis of a Non-Fictional Text, p. 22
→ Prep Course *kompakt*, Basic Types of Non-Fictional Texts, p. 8

 5. With a partner, describe and explain the cartoon on page 76. How does the message of the cartoon support Monbiot's harsh criticism of mankind's behaviour?
→ Prep Course *kompakt*, Analysis of Visuals, p. 30

⫸⫸⫸⫸⫸ **ACTIVITIES** ⫸⫸⫸⫸⫸

6. Are humans really such pigs that pollute and destroy the whole planet and do not care about anything? What about the Green Party movement and millions of people who support organic food and textiles, try to live sustainably?
Compile and present information and graphics that visualize an alternative version to Monbiot's gloomy perspective of man's doom.

Tip: A good and convincing presentation should consist of several elements:
● a short speech
● audio-visual material
● a concise handout for each listener that provides the relevant information graphics, etc.

Step 1:
@ Do research on ecological and 'green' trends, organizations, activist groups, etc. and collect information to flesh out and visualize your presentation.

Step 2:
Sort the information and your research results in a mind map to get a better overview.

Tip: Contrast your examples with the negative examples given in the text to show that solutions are possible.

Example:

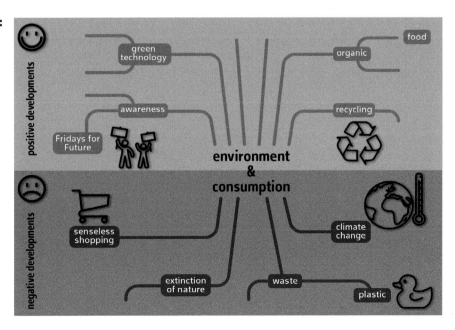

Step 3:

After sorting your ideas, make notes on cards to structure the information and divide your presentation into thematic units.

Tip: Study the respective Skills pages in the supplementary of this book.
→ Prep Course *kompakt*, Presentations, p. 44
→ Prep Course *kompakt*, Giving a Speech, p. 42

Step 4:

Finally, give your presentation, informing the audience about 'green' trends.

Tip: Start your presentation with an 'ice-breaker', an introductory friendly remark that grabs the attention of the audience.
The Tips on vocab box below gives you some ideas.

Tips on vocab 》》》

- Do we really think of ourselves as ignorant 'fools' that do not care about anything?
- Let's use our imagination and think about …
- Human spirit was never limited to …
- Man's intellectual capacity has never shrunk back from … or was limited by …
- Even in the darkest hours of crises human beings were able to …
- Man's capacity to adapt to extreme situations … changes … has made him …
- In nature, nothing is perfect and everything is perfect. Trees can be contorted (*verkrüppelt*), bent in weird ways, and they're still beautiful. (*Alice Walker*)
- Some people walk in the rain, others just get wet. (*Roger Miller*).
- Nature doesn't need people – people need nature; nature would survive the extinction of the human being and go on just fine, but human culture, human beings, cannot survive without nature. (*Harrison Ford*)

GRAMMAR / LANGUAGE ▶▶▶▶▶

7. Extract Monbiot's most relevant arguments and statements from the text. Use **defining and non-defining relative clauses or participle constructions** to give an account of his ideas and thoughts.

Examples:
- The promise of economic growth, which is false, is based on …
- The simple-minded people (who are) depicted in the novel Brave New World, are silenced by …
- It is unbelievable, the global growth rate reached every year, means that …
→ Appendix, Relative Clauses, p. 129
→ Appendix, Participle, p. 127

The Majestic Plastic Bag – A Mockumentary

Worldwide, about one trillion plastic bags are used per year. In the US, the average consumer uses approximately 300 plastic bags per year and a family uses about 15 plastic bags in a single trip to the grocery store. Because of the enormous amount of waste and the many dangers plastic bags pose to the environment, many countries have considered passing new regulations for the production and consumption of plastic bags or even banning them altogether.

 Team up with a partner and study the infographic below. What are the causes of the Great Pacific Garbage Patch, which is actually twice the size of the state of Texas?

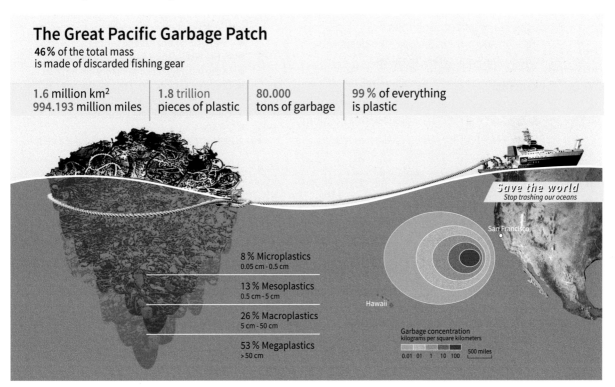

The Great Pacific Garbage Patch
46 % of the total mass
is made of discarded fishing gear

| 1.6 million km²
 994.193 million miles | 1.8 trillion <br> pieces of plastic | 80.000 <br> tons of garbage | 99 % of everything <br> is plastic |

Save the world
Stop trashing our oceans

San Francisco

8 % Microplastics
0.05 cm - 0.5 cm

13 % Mesoplastics
0.5 cm - 5 cm

26 % Macroplastics
5 cm - 50 cm

53 % Megaplastics
> 50 cm

Hawaii

Garbage concentration
kilograms per square kilometers
0.01 0.1 1 10 100   500 miles

 1. Watch the mockumentary *The Majestic Plastic Bag* provided on the webcode and get a first, **general understanding** of the plot.

Webcode SNG-40217-012 @

> Tips on vocab ⟩⟩⟩
>
> **popping ground** here: the place where sth. appears ■ **illustrious** famous ■ **airborne** to be transported by air ■ **to lurk** *lauern* ■ **to encounter** to meet ■ **to lock onto sb./sth.** (*phr. v.*) to find the thing that is being attacked and follow it ■ **deft** skilful and quick ■ **to capture** here: to film or record sth. ■ **weeds** *Unkraut* ■ **branch** *Zweig* ■ **to see to sth.** (*phr. v.*) to deal with sth. ■ **buoyancy** ['bɔɪənsi] here: *Schwimmfähigkeit* ■ **thriving** *gut gehend; blühend* ■ **veritable** (*humorous*) impressive ■ **indefinitely** never-ending

 2. Watch the mockumentary **a second time** and do the comprehension tasks on worksheet 12.1.

SNG-40217-012 @
Worksheet 12.1

3. Summarize the journey of the plastic bag on its way to completing the plastic cycle of life in about 200 words.
   → Prep Course *kompakt*, Writing a Summary, p. 62

   Tip: Keep in mind that the verb 'summarize' requires you to
   ● leave out details,
   ● be as precise and specific as possible,
   ● avoid wordy explanations,
   ● use direct (reported) speech and/or paraphrase,
   ● use predominantly the simple present.

   Tip: Remember to write an introductory sentence that contains
   ● the title, the type of text and the running time of the film/video clip,
   ● the author's/director's name,
   ● the year of publication/release,
   ● the problem/topic the text/film deals with,
   ● important characters/features.

   Example:
   The ironic mockumentary *The Majestic Plastic Bag* released on YouTube in … deals with a fictitious plastic bag's journey from … to …

   Tips on vocab »»»
   ■ The narrator depicts the setting …
   ■ In the first/second part of the journey …
   ■ In the introductory/main/concluding part …
   ■ Despite the dangers … the plastic bag …
   ■ Eventually the plastic bag has to cope with …
   ■ On its journey the bag encounters …
   ■ Finally, …

ANALYSIS

4. Examine the style of the mockumentary and explain its function and effect. Pay attention to the narrative and cinematic devices that are employed as well as the information given in the Info box below.
   → Prep Course *kompakt*, Analysis of a Film Scene, p. 20
   → Prep Course *kompakt*, Camera Operations, p. 14

   Info »»»

   A **mockumentary** (a combination of the words *mock* and *documentary*) is a type of film in which fictional events are presented in a documentary style to create a parody.
   Mockumentaries are often used to comment on or criticize current events, e. g. by following people as they go through various events. Dramatic techniques are combined with documentary elements to depict events as if they were real. Mockumentaries are often improvised to maintain the pretence of reality.

ACTIVITIES

5. **Prepare and act out a panel discussion in which you exchange your views and opinions about plastic bags and how to cope with and solve the problem of plastics waste in general.**

   Step 1:
   @ Do further research on
   a) the Great Pacific Garbage Patch,
   b) how marine animals suffer from plastic waste,
   c) the dangers of (micro) plastics for the food chain,
   d) facts and data concerning the production of plastics.

Step 2:

Divide the class into six groups, each group representing one particular view on "plastics":

- representatives of a supermarket chain
- representatives of a marine animal rescue station
- producers of plastic containers for food
- customers
- politicians
- environmentalists

Step 3:

Each group prepares a short presentation to introduce and explain their position to the class.

Tip: Remember to provide additional visuals, samples and/or a handout for the listeners. Try to be as objective as possible and do not evaluate by employing judgmental adjectives like 'shocking', 'inhuman', 'appalling', etc.

→ Prep Course *kompakt*, Presentations, p. 44

Step 4:

Before starting the discussion, prepare role cards and take notes on the possible pros and cons of the matter. Additionally, select and note down phrases that you will need for the discussion.

Worksheet 12.2 provides you with a set of role cards and the first ideas for your argumentation.

> **Tips on vocab** ≫≫
>
> in my opinion/view ■ that's why ■ it's a fact that ■ another reason is ■ for example ■ you can't deny ■ you can't ignore the fact that ■ on the one hand … on the other (hand) ■ I (don't) go along with ■ I'd/I wouldn't support the view that ■ you disregard the fact that ■ you have … out of consideration ■ in answer to that point ■ basically, that means ■ let me explain again ■ may I come in here ■ there is no denying that ■ to put it more clearly ■ what I'd like to say is

Step 5:

Act out the panel discussion and exchange your views and arguments.

GRAMMAR / LANGUAGE ≫≫≫≫

6. Following the panel discussion, write a newspaper article of about 250 words which contains the different views and opinions expressed in the discussion.
   Choose **adverbs** from the grid below and add them to your formulations. Be careful to put them in the right position.

Examples:
- <u>Yesterday</u> we were able to watch a very heated and controversial discussion about …
- Representatives of a marine animal rescue station <u>repeatedly</u> referred to the <u>extremely</u> dangerous impact of … on …

adverbs of manner	adverbs of frequency	adverbs of place	adverbs of time	adverbs of degree	sentence adverbs
well	never	here	yesterday	extremely	(un-)fortunately
beautifully	always	there	today	hardly	undoubtedly
happily	often	everywhere	tomorrow	very	luckily probably
quickly	sometimes	up	now	quite	generally
enthusiastic	usually	down	then	rather	admittedly
heavily	twice	inside	yet	completely	
cheaply	repeatedly	outside	already	considerably	
cheerfully	just	in England …	at … o'clock	totally	
successfully	eventually	in India …	in the evening	constantly	
sadly	regularly		on May 22, …	absolutely	
deliberately			all day		
			last year		

SNG-40217-012
Worksheet 12.2

Simon Hage et al

Living Sustainably:
Can We Save the Planet Without Having to Do Without?

Step 1: Look at the cover of the 2019 July issue of the German magazine *Der Spiegel*, which was published at the beginning of the German summer vacation season. What image of the 'average German' does the cover convey?

Step 2: Discuss the question asked in the caption.
- Is living 'right' <u>and</u> 'good' (= pleasantly, satisfactorily) morally and ethically (still) possible?
- What is <u>your</u> understanding of a 'good' life?

Step 3: The headline of the article poses the controversial question as to whether (or not) living sustainably and saving the world <u>and</u> living one's life to the fullest is possible.
Try to anticipate what the article's answers might be. What aspects/problems/trends do you expect the authors will focus on? Discuss.

 Many in Germany are trying to do their part to slow climate change. They are conscientious[1] about the purchases[2] they make, they ride bikes and they try to reduce their trash and carbon footprint.
5 They can't solve the problem on their own, but they could force politicians and businesses to act.
Saving the planet isn't going to be easy. It'll take effort[3]. Like packing children's lunches into recycled glass jars[4] and wrapping them in wool socks to prevent them from
10 shattering in kids' backpacks. Or making homemade detergent[5] out of curd soap[6], soda and water. Whatever it takes to avoid plastic packaging. The Meuser family has been living this way for half a year.
"We're only taking small steps, but that alone feels so
15 liberating," says Maik Meuser, 42. "But we also have to invest time and energy," says Nicole Kallwies-Meuser, 41.
Both work full-time. He's a TV host and she's a project manager. They have three children. Their day-to-day
20 family commitments[7] are challenging enough as it is, but at the beginning of the year, the parents asked themselves: How can we leave behind a world for our children that is worth living in and beautiful? Because if something doesn't change soon, the Meusers thought,
25 it's over. And not only for them, but all of humanity.
Surveys show that nearly three-quarters of all Germans are worried about their planet's future. It's no wonder then, that the secretary general of the United Nations

DER SPIEGEL

Nr. 29 / 13.7 2019
Deutschland € 5,30

Richtig und **gut leben**
Die Welt retten, ohne sich einzuschränken – geht das?

Diesel, Maut, Bahn
Die CSU stürzt ein
Ministerium ins Chaos

AfD-Machtkampf
Warum die Radikalen
gewinnen

Zeckenplage
Neue Mittel gegen
die Blutsauger

hardly misses an opportunity to call climate change the "greatest systematic threat to humanity."
30 What's new is this: There is an increasing amount of people like the Meusers who are not only worried but

---

[1] **conscientious** putting a lot of effort into your work; *gewissenhaft* – [2] **purchase** (*fml.*) the act of buying sth. – [3] **effort** *Mühe* – [4] **jar** *Einmachglas, Konservenglas* – [5] **detergent** *Waschmittel* – [6] **curd soap** *Kernseife* – [7] **commitment** *Engagement, Einsatz*

are seriously looking for ways to change the way they live. These are people who have decided that saving the
35 environment isn't merely[8] the purview[9] of the hippy-dippy-granola crowd[10], but for everyone. [...]

2 A new dynamic has emerged, primarily because the climate issue is largely perceived[11] as a question of jus-
40 tice – intergenerational justice. Millions of young people have understood that their future is at stake[12] and that one day they'll pay the price if something doesn't change soon.

"'Fridays for Future' has developed more political power
45 than Greenpeace on its best day," Welzer says. "The process of cultural change that has begun is palpable[13]."

On the other hand, this will to change isn't reflected in figures everywhere. Meat consumption in Germany, for one, hasn't declined[14] at all, even though many people
50 now express a wish to live vegan[15]. And despite the fact that sustainable tourism is en vogue at the moment, just as many Germans fly to their vacation destinations as ever before.

How does this all fit together?
55 The Germans, it seems, were long a people of "climate-concerned climate sinners," the German Federal Environment Agency states. They buy organic sausages, put them in their reusable jute[16] bags and drive home in their SUVs. [...]

Clean Travel?

"Which form of transportation do you intend to use for vacation travel in 2019?"

Car	**55%**
Plane	**40**
Train	**16**
Bus	**7**

Poll conducted by market research institute YouGov for LichtBlick in April and May; 2,525 people surveyed; multiple answers were possible

---

Companies are struggling with similar issues in other
60 industries as well. They want to – and have to – offer more environmentally friendly products. But so far, most of them remain niche[17] offerings. As great as consumer pressure is on the one hand, on the other, it's
65 hard to change consumers' behavior. Everything is supposed to become more sustainable and more ecological – but please, don't let it become at all uncomfortable or unaffordable[18].

The coffee chain Starbucks declared nearly a decade ago that it wanted to replace all of its disposable paper card-
70 board cups with reusable ones. Then in 2015, its goal was to have at least a quarter of all Starbucks cups used in the United States be reusable. In 2018, only 1.8 percent were. This begs the question: If consumers won't voluntarily forgo[19] cardboard cups, why not slap[20] them with a
75 mandatory[21] surcharge[22]? [...]

3 In no other industry, however, does sustainability appear to be as big a deal as in the textile industry. One reason is because there are few industries that are dirtier. Textile manufacturers emitted more than 1.2 billion
80 tons of greenhouse gases in 2015 – more than all international flights and global shipping combined. What's more: 63 percent of all materials used in clothing production are plastic.

According to a recent study by the management con-
85 sulting firm McKinsey, nearly 80 percent of buyers of fashion chains are now operating under the assumption that sustainability will have a major influence on consumer purchasing decisions in the coming years, especially in mass fashion. McKinsey predicts that sustain-
90 ability will be at "the center of innovation in the fashion industry." [...]

4 **The Highest Hurdles Are Psychological**

This means that the highest hurdles today are psychological rather than ideological. "People change their be-
95 havior when the effort requires the least psychologically and financially," says Renn. Swapping[23] plastic bags for cloth bags, for example. [...]

When it comes to sustainable behavior, Grünewald says the average German shows a very clear tendency. "Peo-
100 ple are conflicted: They want to protect the environment, but plastic bags are just so convenient[24]." The

---

[8] **merely** only; and nothing more – [9] **purview** (fml.) Zuständigkeitsbereich – [10] **hippy-dippy-granola crowd** (infml.) durchgeknallte Müsli essende Leute – [11] **to perceive** to understand or think of sb./sth. in a particular way – [12] **at stake** in danger of being lost – [13] **palpable** so obvious that can be easily seen or known – [14] **to decline** to gradually become less, worse or lower – [15] **vegan** a person who does not eat or use any animal products, such as meat, fish, eggs, cheese or leather – [16] **jute** [dʒuːt] – [17] **niche** [niːʃ] affecting only a small number of people – [18] **unaffordable** unerschwinglich – [19] **to forgo** (fml.) to not do or have anything enjoyable – [20] **to slap sb.** jdn. klatschen – [21] **mandatory** verpflichtend – [22] **surcharge** an extra amount of money – [23] **to swap** to exchange – [24] **convenient** praktisch

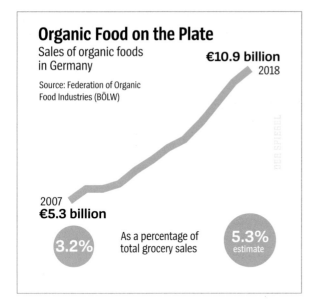

Organic Food on the Plate
Sales of organic foods in Germany

Source: Federation of Organic Food Industries (BÖLW)

€10.9 billion
2018

2007
€5.3 billion

3.2%

As a percentage of total grocery sales

5.3%
estimate

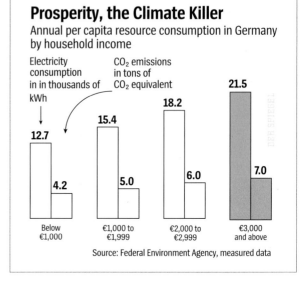

Prosperity, the Climate Killer
Annual per capita resource consumption in Germany by household income

Electricity consumption in in thousands of kWh

CO_2 emissions in tons of CO_2 equivalent

	12.7	15.4	18.2	21.5
Below €1,000	4.2			
€1,000 to €1,999		5.0		
€2,000 to €2,999			6.0	
€3,000 and above				7.0

Source: Federal Environment Agency, measured data

easiest way to resolve[25] this inner strife[26] would be to force them to change their behavior. "That's why people
105 want bans – so they don't have to rely on self-discipline."
In other words: Consumers do best when they have no other choice but the alternative. "Germans have the habit of following these kinds of rules particularly con-
110 scientiously – you can already see that with recycling," says Grünewald. [...]

5 Does Climate Protection Have to Remain a Luxury Good?
It's actually pretty simple: Things that damage the cli-
115 mate should be expensive. There are plenty of scientific studies available on how to get people to change their behavior. One thing pops up again and again: As soon as it hits their pocketbooks[27], even people with the most entrenched[28] behaviors are willing to change. If the hol-
120 iday flight to Thailand no longer costs 800 euros, but 5,000 euros, then people would probably prefer to take a train to the Alps in Bavaria. So, what are we waiting for? Politicians should simply impose[29] proper[30] eco-taxes on everything that harms the environment so that
125 companies make their products more sustainable. If they cost more, then we, as consumers, will just all have to pay more. It would be reasonable to demand that in order to save the planet. [...]

6 Sustainability Needs to Be Fair
That's why the first and most important hurdle that 130 needs to be cleared if we are really serious about finding the path to a more sustainable society is to make sure that it is fair – not only for moral reasons, but also for purely practical ones. "People with lower incomes will only join in if they feel that poor and rich are equally 135 burdened," says Renn. He says this has been a repeat finding in numerous studies he has conducted. In other words: Nothing will come of saving the planet if sustainability is affordable for the upper middle class, but not for those in the lower strata[31] of society. There can 140 be no climate protection without climate solidarity. [...]
The only problem is that the poorer strata in Germany already consume much less than the rich, anyway. In 2016, the UBA[32] prepared a study on "Per Capita Consumption of Natural Resources in Germany." It essen- 145 tially states that, "the higher the education and income, the greater the consumption of resources." The highest total energy consumption is also found in the upper strata, "since they generally have above-average incomes and a lifestyle geared toward[33] status and owner- 150 ship." On average, members of the "simple, vulnerable[34] strata" have the lowest total energy consumption.
In short: If there's a certain group destroying the climate, it's the high-earning, college-educated people who are fond of[35] showing the world to their children 155

---

[25] **to resolve** to end a problem or difficulty – [26] **strife** (*fml.*) violent disagreement – [27] **pocketbook** a woman's handbag – [28] **entrenched** established firmly so that it cannot be changed – [29] **to impose** etw. erheben (Steuern, Gebühren) – [30] **proper** real, suitable – [31] **stratum** Gesellschaftsschicht – [32] **UBA** (abbr.) Umweltbundesamt – [33] **to gear sth. toward** etw. ausrichten auf – [34] **vulnerable** verletzlich – [35] **to be fond of sb./sth.** to like sb./sth. very much

during summer vacation, own two cars as well as a Vespa for the summer and have to heat a 200-square meter (2,152 square feet) apartment in the winter.

[7] Ultimately[36], the question is this: How can the poor
160 and the rich live more sustainably, without a reduction in their current quality of life? And how can we maintain our system of economic growth without being so destructive? It's a bit like the Meusers, the family from Dormagen trying to eliminate plastic from their lives.
165 Their children are still allowed to eat ice cream, even if it comes packed in plastic. Otherwise, their enthusiasm

would dissipate[37] rapidly. Or like the Henkes in Giessen: As long they can't afford an electric car, they will likely keep driving one with a combustion engine[38].

It's a complicated way of life, and there will be fierce[39] 170 debate about many things on the path to sustainability. But the first step is simple, as Welzer, the expert on society with a special feel for Germans' nature, emphasizes. "Just stop whining[40] and start doing something."

Simon Hage, Anton Rainer, Thomas Schulz, Gerald Traufetter, https://www.spiegel.de/international/sustainability-can-we-save-the-planet-without-having-to-do-without-a-1277789.html, 18 July 2019 [19.07.2019]

COMPREHENSION ››››››

1. The article has already been subdivided into seven parts for you. Divide your class into seven groups/teams, each one dealing with one of the parts.
Take notes on your respective part of the text and clarify the questions below in your group.

[1]
- Present how many Germans have changed their lives so far.
- Describe how the Meuser family tries to live sustainably.

[2]
- State what is meant by "the new dynamic".
- Outline the problem that Germans are "climate-concerned climate sinners" and how companies deal with the situation.

[3]
- Specify the problem posed by the textile industry.
- Point out which future trends are to be expected concerning customers of fashion chains.

[4]
- Point out the "psychological dilemma" many people are in.
- Present what needs to be done to persuade consumers to change their behaviour.

[5]
- Describe the author's idea about "expensive things".
- Point out the consequences that environmentally harmful behaviour should have.

[6]
- State the author's demand for fairness.
- Specify the reasons why "the rich" are destroying the climate.

[7]
- Point out the essential questions the author asks regarding the gap between rich and poor.
- State what – according to the author – should be done to make Germans live more sustainably.

Next, change groups, with each group consisting of one member of the former group. In this new group, each member informs the others about the results from their first group.

ANALYSIS ››››››

2. Each new group chooses one of the paragraphs and analyses the stylistic and rhetorical devices* and explains how they help to depict the controversial issue. Focus particularly on:
- the line of argument*
- the use of references and examples
- the use of (rhetorical) questions*
- the use of contrast/antithesis*
→ Prep Course *kompakt*, Analysis of a Non-Fictional Text, p. 22

[36]**ultimately** in the end – [37]**to dissipate** (*fml.*) to gradually disappear – [38]**combustion engine** *Verbrennungsmotor* – [39]**fierce** powerful, frightening – [40]**to whine** *jammern*

3. Analyse the graph and the bar charts (pp. 83 and 84) and relate them to the article:
   a) What do the Germans' choices of transportation reveal about their eco-friendliness?
   b) Describe the pattern of Germans' grocery purchases?
   c) Explain the connection between resource consumption and income in Germany.
   → Prep Course *kompakt*, Analysis of Statistical Data, p. 28

ACTIVITIES

4. At least since the record heat wave in the summer of 2018 and the emerging *Fridays for Future* initiative, more and more people are concerned about climate change and its impact.
Faced with the new developments, you and your friends have organized a youth conference and invited various experts and people with experience on the matter.
You have been asked to give the introductory speech to the conference, in which you describe the situation, outline the controversy about how to react and motivate those attending the youth conference to take action.

Step 1:
You can use the information given in the article (and the attached statistics), but you should also do further research on
@
- climate change/global warming,
- the impact of climate change on flora and fauna,
- statements and assessments from experts.

Sort your findings in the following categories, which you can use for your speech later on.

information/facts	impact of climate change	action taken so far
● 75 % of Germans are worried about … ● 1.2 billion tons of …	● carbon footprint … ● …	● avoiding packaging … ● …

Step 2:
Prepare your speech and select the aspects and information you want to talk about. As you are expected to speak in favour of environmental protection and against using plastic, too much waste, etc. your speech should have a clear line of argument in which you present the problems, the pros and cons as well as possible solutions – but finally come to the conclusion that the disadvantages of plastics, etc. outweigh the possible benefits.

Tip: Outline your argumentative strategy in an overview and collect and sort your arguments like this:

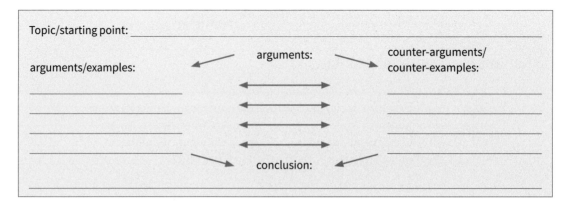

→ Prep Course *kompakt*, Basic Types of Non-Fictional Texts, p. 8

Step 3:

Bear in mind that your speech introduces the conference. So you should make some welcoming remarks first:

a) introducing the invited guests and experts to the participants/audience

b) thanking your guests/experts for coming and sharing their knowledge with you

Additionally, think of a good introduction to the subject of the conference to make your listeners aware of the problem and arouse their interest.

You can, for example, use the *Spiegel* front cover (p. 82) or the cartoon (below) to illustrate the controversy.

Tips on vocab ⟫

> ■ Dear friends, ladies and gentlemen, distinguished guests and experts …
> ■ Let me say how grateful I am to …
> ■ We are so grateful to have you here …
> ■ There is no denying that the situation has become alarming …
> ■ Do we really know what problems our relentless consumption and careless wastefulness is causing?
> ■ Can we really risk …?
> ■ Why are we naive enough to believe that …?

Tips on vocab ⟫

Noah's Ark ■ a pirate impersonating/symbolizing fossil fuels ■ sabre (*Säbel*) ■ animals crammed into the ark ■ penguin ■ chimpanzees ■ giraffes ■ tortoises ■ elephants ■ chamois (*Gämse*) ■ donkeys ■ rhinos ■ flamingo ■ tiger ■ ostrich (*Strauß*) ■ to look scared ■ to pull the corners of one's mouth ■ to have worry lines on one's forehead

Extinction Cruise by Steve Sack, 7 May 2019, in: The Minneapolis Star-Tribune

Step 4:

Make use of the **postcard technique**.

a) Structure your speech by breaking it into sections (sense units),

b) give each section a heading,

c) write one heading and a few easily-read prompt words or some data on each card,

d) think about a logical structure for your speech that makes it easily comprehensible for your listeners,

    → Prep Course *kompakt*, Basic Types of Non-Fictional Texts, p. 8

e) decide on certain formal and stylistic devices that you will employ in your speech in order to make it more appealing and interesting for the audience,

    → Prep Course *kompakt*, Analysis of a Political Speech, p. 26

f) number the cards in the order in which you want to present these points.

Step 5:

Finally, give your speech and convey your point of view to the listeners, according to the following structure:

- Greet the audience and introduce yourself.
- Don't simply read out what's on your cards, your transparency, PowerPoint, etc. but paraphrase and explain them.
- Speak more slowly and loudly than usual.
- Make eye-contact.
- Pause and take a break after each point.
- If you feel comfortable and confident enough, you can ask your audience whether they have any questions.
- At the end, conclude with a concise summary of your topic and a meaningful (= *prägnant*) final sentence or remark.

→ Prep Course *kompakt*, Giving a Speech, p. 42
→ Prep Course *kompakt*, Presentations, p. 44
→ Appendix, Connectives and Adverbs, p. 120

Tip: Additionally, prepare a handout for your listeners that contains the relevant information and gives them an overview of the issue.

 Worksheet 13.1 provides you with a sample for you to use.

> **Tips on vocab** >>>>
> - to face reality
> - to gain a deeper insight of
> - to stop ignoring
> - to quit glossing over
> - an irresponsible denial of risk and reality
> - to ignore potential dangers and risks
> - to turn a blind eye to sth.

GRAMMAR / LANGUAGE >>>>>>>

 5. Reactivate your **vocabulary** in connection with the topic of the environment and sustainability. Complete the vocabulary list provided on worksheet 13.2 and fill in the empty boxes. Use a dictionary for help if necessary.

Noah Haidle
Everything Beautiful

The protagonist of Noah Haidle's play, Cookie Close, is an aging, once successful door-to-door saleswoman who works for the American cosmetics company *Mary Kay*. Mary Kay's business strategy is direct sales, i.e. sales people ("beauty consultants") selling the products directly to customers and getting a commission for what and how much they sell. In the company's strict hierarchy, beauty consultants are on the lowest level but can work their way up the company ladder, according to how successful they are. Depending on their respective position within the company, they must wear certain uniforms and colours (e. g. beauty consultants → pink; sales directors → royal blue).
The scene at hand depicts Cookie Close, who has coincidentally met an old friend of hers, Vera, who has just returned from her husband's funeral service and, understandably, is depressed and emotionally unstable.
a) What impression does the photo convey of Cookie and her "customer", Vera?
b) What do the colours reveal about the overall atmosphere during this scene?

COOKIE
Have you ever thought about trying a new look?

VERA
What's wrong with my look?

5 COOKIE
Nothing!
Oh, God, I didn't mean to say it like that, I meant to say it like, taking agency[1], being in charge of[2] circumstance, seeing yourself for what you are.

10 VERA
And what is that?

COOKIE
Another iteration[3] of God's masterpiece.

VERA
15 What would you suggest I change?

COOKIE
Well.

She opens her rolly bag.
Lots of cosmetics.

20 COOKIE
I might suggest beginning with age fighting moisturizer[4].
Oh certainly foundation primer[5].
Perhaps the ultimate Mascara.

Cookie Close (right) selling cosmetics to Vera (left); photo taken during a theatrical production at Theater Krefeld-Mönchengladbach

Wow, I can't believe I still have the Luminosity[6] Luminizing[7] Set, an impossibly popular item, definitely that. 25
Wrinkle-be-gone[8], who can live without it, am I wrong?
And Lovestruck Cranberry Lipstick.
And the Bedroom Eyes[9] Eyebrow definer pencil.
And the Understated Mask.
And exfoliant[10], pumice stones[11], moisturizer, and final- 30
ly the Standard Bromwich Nail File, the gold standard of nail files.

---

[1] **to take agency** to be in charge of sth. – [2] **to be in charge of sb./sth.** to be responsible for sb./sth. – [3] **iteration** (*fml.*) the process of doing sth. again and again, usually to improve it – [4] **moisturizer** *Feuchtigkeitscreme* – [5] **foundation primer** *Grundierung* – [6] **luminosity** *Brillanz, Leuchtkraft* – [7] **to luminize** to light up – [8] **wrinkle** *Falte, Runzel* – [9] **bedroom eyes** the sensual/seductive look you have when you are in the mood for a romantic and/or sexual experience – [10] **exfoliant** *Peeling* – [11] **pumice stone** *Bimsstein*

VERA
Wow.
35 That's a lot.

COOKIE
Hey sister, tell me about it.
But looking good outside makes you look good inside.
I'm proof!
40 Look at me.
Do you think this amount of togetherness comes easy?
No way, Josie.
Hours every day.
Upkeep[12]!
45 It's endless.
But!
The results, if I might say so myself, are worth the effort.
Michelangelo said that his sculptures were waiting for
him, inside the marble[13], calling to him to let them out.
50 God made us in His own image.
I say let the image out!
So that we might be reminded that we are all His beauti-
ful creatures.
Will these products heal you?
55 No, I'm not promising that, nothing can except time, but
by God you can look good while you're waiting.

VERA
What do I owe you for all these?

COOKIE
60 I can't accept money from you, Vera.
This is on the house.
You're grieving[14].

VERA
Cookie.

COOKIE 65
This is to help you feel beautiful again!
In this time of dire[15] need for it.

VERA
But this inventory[16], it comes out of your pocket.
I know how direct sales[17] works. 70
I insist.

Cookie sighs.

COOKIE
The Ultimate Mascara, Wrinkle Be Gone, the moisturizer, eyebrow pencil, and sleep mask are all $39.99, the 75
lipstick usually goes for $27.99 but I can knock it down
to $23 even, friend prices, the Luminizing set, which I
can't believe I still have in stock, is $179.99, the exfoli-
ant and pumice stones are $18 each, and I'll throw in[18]
the Standard Bromwich Nail File for free, so, with 8% 80
sales tax brings the grand total to $474.05, but for effi-
ciency[19] and to honor our shared history, let's just say
$474.

VERA
Wow. 85

COOKIE
That's the price of beauty!

VERA
Let me just go inside and get my purse.

COOKIE 90
I'll wait!!

Everything Beautiful by Noah Haidle. Bildungshaus Schulbuchverlage,
Braunschweig, 2019, pp. 23 ff. © Noah Haidle, 2018

>>>> **COMPREHENSION** >>>>>>>

1. After reading the scene, find evidence from the text that supports the statement:
"Cookie: I don't sell cosmetics, I sell beauty!"

2. While reading the scene **a second time**, find sentences that match the following statements.
Note: There are more aspects listed than can be found in the text.
a) Vera's looks do not reveal her inner self.
b) Cosmetics highlight God's masterpiece.
c) Vera appears to be relatively old.

[12] **upkeep** the cost or process of keeping sb./sth. in good condition – [13] **marble** *Marmor* – [14] **to grieve** to feel or express great sadness,
esp. when sb. dies – [15] **dire** very serious or extreme – [16] **inventory** the total amount of goods in stock – [17] **direct sales** a sale that is made
directly to the customer and not through a store; Direktverkauf – [18] **to throw in** to include sth. with what you are selling, without increasing the price – [19] **efficiency** *Effizienz*; here: *Zeitersparnis*

d) Luminizers help to brighten up faces.

e) Vera's skin reveals that she is old and tired.

f) You can only feel good if you look good.

g) Women are like Michelangelo's statues.

h) Cookie spends a lot of time putting on her makeup.

i) Cookie wants to emotionally support Vera.

j) Makeup helps to bring out women's true image.

k) Vera knows how poor Cookie is.

l) Cookie helps Vera because they are old friends.

m) Cookie offers Vera a special discount.

n) Vera is ashamed by Cookie's generous offer.

ANALYSIS

SNG-40217-014 **3.** Examine Cookie's sales strategy and how she praises and promotes her products. Use worksheet 14.1
Worksheet 14.1 for your analysis.

SNG-40217-014 @ **4.** Analyse the course of the dialogue: How does Cookie lure (*locken*) Vera into buying her cosmetic prod-
Worksheet 14.2 ucts? Worksheet 14.2 provides you with the respective material.
→ Prep Course *kompakt*, Analysis of a Fictional Text, p. 18

5. Characterize Cookie's behaviour – is she the good friend she pretends to be? How does she treat Vera?
→ Prep Course *kompakt*, Characterization of a Figure in Literature, p. 34

6. Compare Cookie's behaviour to advertising (strategies) in real life.
- How does advertising use or abuse the emotional condition of people?
- Have you ever been lured into buying sth. because you were sad/frustrated/happy?

7. Examine and explain the statistical data on best-selling cosmetic products and the top cosmetic compa-
nies worldwide (below and on p. 92).
- What are the sales and product strategies?
- Who are the global leaders in beauty sales?
→ Prep Course *kompakt*, Analysis of Statistical Data, p. 28

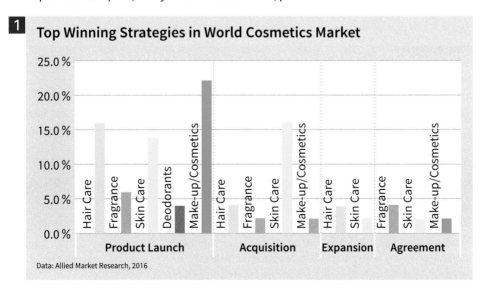

1 **Top Winning Strategies in World Cosmetics Market**

Data: Allied Market Research, 2016

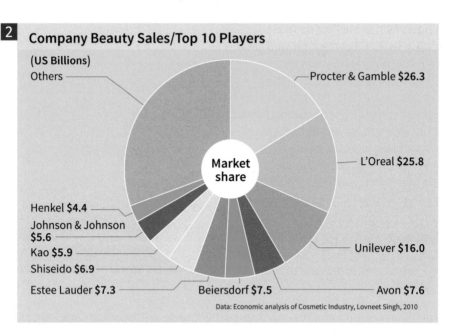

2 **Company Beauty Sales/Top 10 Players**

(US Billions)

Market share

- Others
- Procter & Gamble $26.3
- L'Oreal $25.8
- Unilever $16.0
- Avon $7.6
- Beiersdorf $7.5
- Estee Lauder $7.3
- Shiseido $6.9
- Kao $5.9
- Johnson & Johnson $5.6
- Henkel $4.4

Data: Economic analysis of Cosmetic Industry, Lovneet Singh, 2010

ACTIVITIES >>>>>>>>

8. Environmental activists in cooperation with the Green Party have launched a campaign addressed particularly to young people which wants to inform them about and warn them against the enormous increase of cosmetics products and their environmental and health risks.
   They conduct interviews with teenagers from different backgrounds to find out more about their
   a) shopping habits and preferences for particular cosmetic products,
   b) willingness to buy less,
   c) economic/financial background and how much they spend on cosmetics,
   d) interest and knowledge of the harmful environmental impact of cosmetics,
   e) knowledge of animal experiments to develop and test cosmetic products.

   Tip: Use the information given in the statistics for more specific and investigative questions.

Step 1:
Make some short notes on topics and background information you would like to interview the respective person about, e. g.
- what (further) information and personal experiences they can add to the matter,
- what specific experiences they have made with certain cosmetics,
- their personal view of (certain) cosmetic products,
- etc.

Step 2:
Now, formulate your questions.

Tip: Use the information given on how to formulate questions in the Info box in Skill 5, p. 41.

Examples:
- Which cosmetic products do you use?
- What do you like or dislike about cosmetics?
- What makes you buy or want to buy certain products?
- How environmentally-friendly are the products you buy?

Step 3:

After having written down a number of questions, put yourself in the position of the respondent and think about possible answers that might reflect the person's situation and position.

Tip: In order to make the interview more realistic, employ linguistic devices and communicative strategies such as

- 'fillers',
- feedback phrases to emphasize that you are listening closely,
- friendly comments to create a good and conciliatory atmosphere,
- turn-taking phrases to bring in another person,
- avoiding judgmental comments,
- expressing yourself indirectly by using conditional forms,
- making a pause after a statement,
- using question tags,
- making suggestions.
→ Prep Course *kompakt*, Conversation and Discussion, p. 38
→ Appendix, Connectives and Adverbs, p. 120

> **Tips on vocab – fillers** ▶▶▶
>
> last but not least ■ in answer to that point ■ in general ■ to put it more clearly ■ it seems obvious to me that ■ it appears to be evident ■ what I'd like to say is

Tip: Be careful not to overdo and use too many fillers – you do not want to produce empty phrases.

GRAMMAR / LANGUAGE ▶▶▶▶

9. A major cosmetics company wants to know about the satisfaction of their customers with their products. Therefore, they send out interviewers to personally ask customers about their opinion.

Team up with a partner and act out these interviews about the specific likes and dislikes concerning cosmetic products you use.

Use **adverbial clauses of time, reason, result, purpose, conclusion and contrast** for your questions and answers. Choose adverbs from the grid below and add them to your formulations. Be careful to put them in the right position.

Examples:
- Even though the lotion was expensive, it didn't have any effect on my skin.
- Have you ever bought a cosmetic product because it was advertised?

adverbs of time	adverbs of reason	adverbs of result	adverbs of purpose	adverbs of conclusion	adverbs of contrast
now then today tomorrow annually daily nightly weekly yearly before meanwhile	hence therefore	such so … that so much that in order that such that	since so thus therefore	definitely once and for all positively finally decisively	although though even though even if while whereas however despite in spite of on the other hand rather but nevertheless

→ Appendix, Adjectives and Adverbs, p. 115

Resulting from excessive production, the irresponsible handling and disposal of articles made of plastic has become a major threat to the environment as well as to animals and humans alike. This has led to an ongoing debate about how to tackle this disaster.

Angela Hengsberger
Warum Kleidung aus Plastikmüll nicht für saubere Meere sorgen kann

G-Star kooperiert mit Musik-Star Pharrell Williams

Die niederländische Jeansmarke G-Star hat [...] mit Parley und dem Künstler Pharrell Williams Kleidung[1] aus
5 Plastikabfällen entwickelt. Das von Williams geförderte[2] BioTech-Startup Bionic Yarn schafft den Plastikmüll aus dem Meer, der wiederum als Rohstoff[3] für die *Raw for the Oceans*-Kollektion dient. Die Kooperation war derart erfolgreich, dass Pharrell Williams mittlerweile
10 Miteigentümer[4] von G-Star geworden ist.

Aus alten Fischernetzen[5] werden Bademode[6] oder Strümpfe[7]
Nicht nur große, bekannte Labels nutzen Plastikabfälle, um neue Kleidung herzustellen. Auch ganz junge und
15 kleine Marken upcyclen Müll aus dem Meer. Die 2015 von Barbara Gölles und Andrea Kollar gegründete Bademodenbrand *Margaret and Hermione* nutzt Fischernetze, die im Meer treiben[8] und dort Schaden anrichten, als Ausgangsstoff für ihre Kollektion. Die Netze werden zu-
20 nächst zu Garn[9] und weiter zu Bademodestoffen verarbeitet.
Kunert, Strumpfspezialist aus Immenstadt im Allgäu, bietet seit Januar 2017 Feinstrumpfhosen[10] an, die zu 100 Prozent aus alten Fischernetzen gemacht sind. Roh-
25 stoff für die Textilien ist dabei die Garnneuheit Econyl. Dieses Nylon-Garn, das aus Plastikabfällen aus dem Meer gewonnen wird, hat einen weiteren Vorteil: Es kann unendlich[11] oft recycelt werden, wie der italienische Hersteller Aquafil verspricht.

30 Ein Lebenszyklus ohne Ende
Genau diese Eigenschaft des Garns wird in Zukunft für alle Rohstoffe eine wichtige Rolle spielen müssen: ein Produkt kann künftig nicht mehr einen Lebenszyklus[12] mit einem Ende haben. Das Müllproblem lässt sich
35 nachhaltig[13] nämlich nur lösen, wenn dieses Ende gleichzeitig der Anfang für ein neues, genauso hochwertiges[14] Produkt ist. Anders gesagt: Wenn aus Pet-Flaschen T-Shirts hergestellt werden und diese T-Shirts

am Ende auch wieder Restmüll[15] sind, dann löst dieser Weg das Abfallproblem nicht. Diese Tatsache betonte 40 etwa auch Andreas Röhrich, Leiter der Entwicklungsabteilung[16] des internationalen Wäscheherstellers Wolford, in einem Interview mit LEAD Innovation. Wolford arbeitet gemeinsam mit 11 anderen Firmen an einem kompostierbaren[17] BH[18]. Dieses Produkt, dem 2019 eine 45 ganze Wäschelinie folgen soll, wird aber nicht nur nach seinem Lebenszyklus zu wertvollem Kompost[19]. Retourniert der Kunde die Textilien, dann kann ein Garnhersteller [...] [daraus] wieder ein Polymer machen, das als Rohstoff für ein neues Textilteil dient. 50

Von der Wiege zurück zur Wiege
Cradle-to-Cradle nennt sich dieser Ansatz. Dieses Konzept ist nichts geringeres als die Vision einer völlig abfallfreien Wirtschaft, in der gesundheits- oder umweltschädigende[20] Stoffe keine Verwendung mehr finden. 55 Alle Materialien sollen sich entweder in den natürlichen Kreislauf reintegrieren lassen (so wie bei der Kompostierung[21] von Unterwäsche). Oder aber, Rohstoffe wie Metall oder eben Kunststoff, lassen sich unendlich oft für den gleichen Zweck verwenden. [...] 60

Fazit: Warum Kleidung aus Plastikmüll nicht für saubere Meere sorgen kann
Anders als Glas oder Metall war Plastik von Anfang an als Rohstoff für den Einweg-Gebrauch[22] gedacht. Seit der Erfindung des vielseitig verwendbaren Materials haben 65 sich jedoch imposante Müllberge angesammelt, von denen ein großer Teil auf und im Meer schwimmt. Diesen Müll wieder zu verwerten, ist ein löblicher Ansatz. Selbiger hilft allerdings nur dann weiter, wenn aus einer Wiederverwertung eine Immerwiederverwertung wird. Die 70 Kunststoffindustrie wird sich also möglichst bald zu einer Kreislaufwirtschaft wandeln. Dass dies machbar ist, zeigen bereits erste Erfolge, wie der kompostierbare BH von Wolford oder auch die Faser Econyl.

https://www.lead-innovation.com/blog/warum-kleidung-aus-
plastikm%C3%BCll-nicht-f%C3%BCr-saubere-meere-sorgen-kann,
12 September 2018 [08.01.2020]

ℳ **1.** Mediate the online-article above which was published by Lead Innovation Management, a Germany-based marketing and management agency.

Tip: You will possibly need the information given in the article for the debate later on.

[1] apparel – [2] to promote – [3] raw material – [4] co-owner – [5] fishing net – [6] beach fashion – [7] hosiery – [8] to drift – [9] yarn – [10] pantihose – [11] indefinitely – [12] lifecycle – [13] sustainable – [14] premium – [15] residual waste – [16] research and development (R&D) – [17] compostable – [18] brassiere, bra – [19] compost – [20] environmentally damaging – [21] composting – [22] single use, disposable use

Ocean. Now!

In Your Face: 50 Beaches – 50 Faces

In Your Face is a collective project with international participants. Over five months, ocean lovers collected microplastic samples which are now presented as a 'beauty mask' on the faces of well-known people. The project's plan is to ban microplastics in cosmetics and cleaning products.

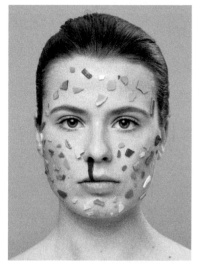

Was bedeutet dir der Ozean?

Dieter:
Plastik gehört ebenso wenig ins Meer wie Senf und Ketchup in einen Teller Milchreis.

Luisa:
Wem das Klima am Herzen liegt, kommt an den Ozeanen nicht vorbei. Klimaschutz heißt auch Meeresschutz.

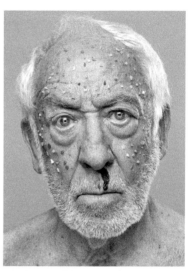

Luisa Neubauer, Aktivistin bei
#FridaysForFuture Deutschland

Dieter Hallervorden – Schauspieler,
Theaterleiter

2. Organize and prepare a debate on the controversial issue of how to deal with microplastics.

 Step 1: Divide the class into different groups, with each group representing a specific viewpoint.

- the car industry
- the packaging industry
- environmentalists/climate activists
- marine researchers
- doctors
- the petrochemical industry

 Step 2: In your group, do research on your chosen topic, collecting information for your argumentation.

 Step 3: Remember that a debate is a formal type of discussion with a specific structure and strict rules. Use the aspects given in the checklist for your preparation.

Checklist

elements ...	function ...

• form debate teams
• choose a moderator
	→ each team has to take a clear position
	  a) stating arguments in favour of sth.
	  b) challenging the arguments of the other side
	  c) substantiating its own position with arguments for or against the resolution

• each team names a first speaker	→ avoiding chaos → supporting clearly structured statements
• each team's speaker gives an opening statement	→ clarifying the topic and viewpoint
• the moderator monitors the time allowed to debaters • the moderator takes questions from the audience	→ providing clear structure and order → focusing on the essentials
• each team's speaker holds a two-minute closing argument	→ summing up the topic from their perspective → appealing to the audience
• the audience makes a final vote/decision	

East, West, Home's Best? – Culture & Identity

Discarded Humanity by Patrick Chappatte, 8 July 2018

Tips on vocab ≫

the globe ▪ huge billboards ▪ on either side of the globe ▪ left: the upper part of Donald Trump's head; right: the logo of the EU ▪ a huge refugee camp ▪ to look like a continent ▪ endless rows of tents ▪ tiny (silhouettes of) people ▪ to be stuck (in between/in the middle of)

START-UP ACTIVITIES

1. Describe the cartoon above. What overall view does the cartoon depict about
   a) the attitudes of the USA and Europe to migration and refugees,
   b) the situation of international refugees and how they are treated?
   → Prep Course *kompakt*, Analysis of Visuals, p. 30

2. What does the bar chart reveal about the origin, the destination (*Ziel*) and the final distribution of migrants? Where are obvious changes and differences?
   → Prep Course *kompakt*, Analysis of Statistical Data, p. 28

United Nations
International Migration Report 2017

In today's increasingly interconnected world, international migration has become a reality that touches nearly all corners of the globe. Modern transportation has made it easier, cheaper and faster for people to
5 move in search of jobs, opportunity, education and quality of life. At the same time, conflict, poverty, inequality and a lack of sustainable livelihoods[1] compel[2] people to leave their homes to seek a better future for themselves and their families abroad.
10 When supported by appropriate policies, migration can contribute to inclusive[3] and sustainable[4] economic growth and development in both home and host communities. In 2016, migrants from developing countries sent home an estimated US $413 billion in remittances[5].
15 Remittances constitute[6] a significant source of household income that improves the livelihoods of families and communities through investments in education, health, sanitation[7], housing and infrastructure. Countries of destination benefit significantly from migra-
20 tion, as migrants often fill critical labour gaps, create

jobs as entrepreneurs[8], and pay taxes and social security contributions. Some migrants are among the most dynamic members of the host society, contributing to the development of science and technology and enrich-
25 ing their host communities by providing cultural diversity.
Despite the significant benefits of migration, some migrants remain among the most vulnerable members of society. Migrants are often the first to lose their jobs in the event of an economic downturn. Some work for less
30 pay, for longer hours, and in worse conditions than native-born workers. While migration is often an empowering[9] experience, some migrants endure[10] human rights violations[11], abuse and discrimination. Migrants, particularly women and children, may fall victim to hu-
35 man trafficking[12] and the heinous[13] forms of exploitation that it entails[14].

https://www.un.org/en/development/desa/population/migration/ publications/migrationreport/docs/MigrationReport2017_Highlights. pdf, pp. 1 f. [25.07.2019]

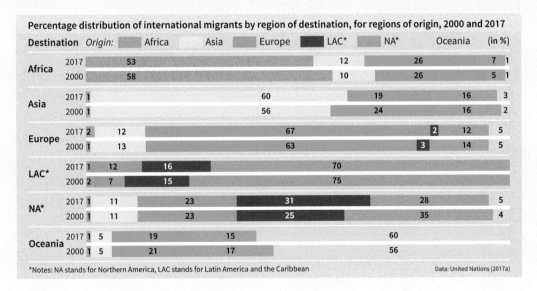

Percentage distribution of international migrants by region of destination, for regions of origin, 2000 and 2017

Destination	Origin:	Africa	Asia	Europe	LAC*	NA*	Oceania	(in %)
Africa	2017	53		12		26	7	1
	2000	58		10		26	5	1
Asia	2017	1	60		19		16	3
	2000	1	56		24		16	2
Europe	2017	2	12	67	2		12	5
	2000	1	13	63	3		14	5
LAC*	2017	1	12	16	70			
	2000	2	7	15	75			
NA*	2017	1	11	23	31		28	5
	2000	1	11	23	25		35	4
Oceania	2017	1	5	19	15	60		
	2000	1	5	21	17	56		

*Notes: NA stands for Northern America, LAC stands for Latin America and the Caribbean   Data: United Nations (2017a)

 3. Together with a partner, find out about
- the causes,
- the risks and benefits of migration as depicted in the UN's 2017 migration report.

[1] **livelihood** the money a person needs to pay for food, a place to live, etc. and the way of earning this money – [2] **to compel** [kəmˈpel] (*fml.*) to force sb. to do sth. – [3] **inclusive** including many different types of people who are treated fairly and equally – [4] **sustainable** *nachhaltig* – [5] **remittance** (*fml.*) an amount of money that you send to sb. – [6] **to constitute** to make sth. up, to form sth. – [7] **sanitation** *sanitäre Anlagen* – [8] **entrepreneur** [ˌɒntrəprəˈnɜːr] sb. who starts their own business – [9] **to empower sb.** to encourage and support the ability to do sth. – [10] **to endure** to face, to experience – [11] **violation** *Verletzung; Nichtbeachtung* – [12] **human trafficking** *Menschenhandel* – [13] **heinous** [ˈheɪnəs] (*fml.*) terrible and shocking – [14] **to entail** (*fml.*) to involve sth.

John Moore

2-Year-Old Yanela Sanchez and Her Mother, Sandra Sanchez

AWARENESS ⟫⟫⟫⟫

On 12 June 2018, photographer John Moore took the now-famous photo of a crying two-year-old girl from Honduras, Yanela Sanchez, while her mother, Sandra, was being checked by a border control agent prior to both mother and child were taken to a processing centre for migrants. Yanela and her mother had just crossed the Rio Grande, hoping to request asylum. In April 2019, John Moore's photo was named the World Press Photo of the Year by an independent jury.

In a Round Robin-activity, express your first impression of the photo and what it means.

Yanela and her mother at the Mexican border, 12 June 2018; photo by John Moore

Tips on vocab ⟫⟫

background: night – dark surrounding background ■ gravel road

left side: huge police car/tyre ■ an inscription and the police logo is partly visible ("US")

centre: small/fragile child ■ pink shirt and pink shoes (eye-catcher) ■ crying/sobbing ■ desperate facial expression ■ tousled hair ■ woman leaning on to police vehicle ■ arms and legs spread

right side: tall police officer ■ carrying a gun ■ handcuffs (*Handschellen*) ■ wearing blue plastic gloves ■ checking the woman's belt

COMPREHENSION ⟩⟩⟩⟩⟩⟩

1. Describe the photograph in detail, paying attention to:
- the overall atmosphere it conveys
- the people, their actions, body language and facial expressions
- the surroundings
- striking eye-catchers and visual symbols

Tip: Use worksheet 15.1 for a precise labelling of details.

Tip: Use the Tips on vocab box on p. 98 and, in a final description of the photo, answer the w-questions (who – what – where – when – why?).
Additionally, think about a particular structure for your description, e. g. from the left to the right, from background to foreground, etc.

ANALYSIS ⟩⟩⟩⟩⟩⟩

2. Analyse the emotional impact as well as the message of the photo by examining its various visual elements and symbols.
→ Prep Course *kompakt*, Analysis of Visuals, p. 30

3. The photo was named the World Press Photo of the Year in 2019. Speculate about the reasons the jury might have selected this photograph from the many taken by professional photographers.

ACTIVITIES ⟩⟩⟩⟩⟩⟩

4. **You are a journalist writing for either a quality or a popular newspaper and are asked to write a story about the photo taken at the Mexican border.**
Write an article/a cover story for a newspaper of your choice that captures the situation and employs additional information on the people and the political background.

Tip: Before writing the article, do further research into the background of the photo and the international reaction to it.

Step 1:
Team up with a partner and decide on the type of newspaper you want to write for and reactivate your knowledge of its specific characteristics.
→ Prep Course *kompakt*, The Press, p. 10

Step 2:
After choosing a particular type of newspaper, think about characteristic features and elements your article should include and complete the grid below.

Alternatively, you can use the grid provided on worksheet 15.2.

	quality newspaper	popular newspaper
characteristics	• informative • critical • …	• sensationalist • emotional • …
elements/components	• research data • …	• banner headlines in bold type • human interest story • …
language	• formal • …	• superlatives • …
photos/visuals	• …	• …

Step 3:

Use a dictionary and find the respective formal and informal synonyms of adjectives, nouns and phrases you want to use in your article.

Usually, the more formal words have more syllables and derive (*abstammen*) from Latin or French. In contrast, many of the everyday words are short.

SNG-40217-015
Worksheet 15.2

You can use the grid provided on worksheet 15.2 for your notes as well.

Examples:

adjectives/nouns/phrases	everyday/informal English	formal English
ängstlich	scared, frightened	
hilflos	helpless	
auf. jdn. zugehen		to approach sb.
helfen	to help	
Hilfe	help	
etc.		

Step 4:

Using a computer, design and type-set the newspaper page on-screen. Think about a layout that matches your chosen newspaper and arrange the necessary elements (e. g. columns of text, photos, an interview, banner headline, etc.) accordingly.

Step 5:

Finally, write the textual elements of your newspaper article, proofread it and make sure to crosscheck the factual information, figures, etc. in order to have valid and correct information. Remember to cite the sources you have used.

➔ Prep Course *kompakt*, Writing a Newspaper Article, p. 58

Tip: In order to flesh out your story with more details and background information on Yanela and her mother, and the reasons for their immigration to the USA and their arrest at the border:
- conduct an interview with Yanela's mother
- conduct an interview with the police officer
- write a human interest story about people who have suffered from crossing the border, being arrested, parents separated from their children, etc.
- appeal to the readers to stand up for migrant rights, human rights, etc.

>>>>> **GRAMMAR / LANGUAGE** >>>>>>>>

5. Replace some of the (overused) **verbs, adjectives and nouns** in the sentences below in order to formulate them more clearly and specifically.
   - Many people from Mexico think that everything is better in America than at home.
   - Sometimes, the police officers are angry and not nice to the refugees.
   - Human rights activists say that the places where Mexicans are taken to are dangerous and dirty.
   - Often, parents and children cannot stay together.
   - Yanela's mother thinks that the police officer is not a good man.

Marina Lewycka

Two Caravans

AWARENESS ⟫⟫⟫⟫⟫

With around 500,000 visitors daily, London's Oxford Street is one of Europe's busiest shopping streets, with massive annual sales. Unfortunately, along with the excellent shopping rates, Oxford Street has suffered from a lot of criminality as well, such as vehicle crime, robberies and many instances of anti-social behaviour. A 2005 police report named Oxford Street as the most dangerous street in Central London.

People shopping in Oxford Street, London

a) Against the background of the information given above and the impression the photograph makes on you, speculate on what makes Oxford Street so appealing and attractive to tourists. Would you want to go there? Why (not)?

b) Whether (or not) you already have been to London yourself, you surely have a certain picture in mind when thinking about it.
Complete the sentence "London is …", expressing your ideas and impressions.

1 When he was thirteen, his father had bought a second-hand sky-blue Zaporozhets 965[1] – the Zaz they called it affectionately, humpbacked[2] like a kind old granddad. It was the first mass-produced workers' car
5 in Ukraine. Real metal body – not fibreboard[3] rubbish like the Trabant[4]. He was the first person in their apartment block to own one. Every Sunday he cleaned and polished it out in the street, and sometimes he and Andriy would spend a couple of hours together, head to
10 head under the bonnet[5], just tinkering[6]. […] He learnt something about car engines, but the main thing he learnt was that all problems can be solved if you approach them in a patient and methodical way. In the end, the car outlived his father. Poor Dad. […]
15 **2** The weather is too warm. Despite the recent rain, the air is clearly dusty again. It smells of fumes and blocked drains[7] and the miscellaneous[8] smells of the five million other people who are breathing at the same time. He feels an unexpected excitement rising in him.
20 This London – once you've got your feet on the ground, and you don't have to worry about those Angliski[9] bandit-drivers – this London is quite something.

He is amazed, at first, just by the vastness of it – the way it goes on and on until you forget there is anything beyond it. OK, he has seen Canterbury and Dover, but noth- 25 ing can prepare you for the sheer[10] excess of this city. Cars that glide as smooth and silent as silver swans, deluxe model, not the battered[11] old smoke-belchers[12] you get back home. Office blocks that almost blot out[13] the sky. And everything in good order – roads, pavements, 30 etc. – all well maintained. But why are all the buildings and statues covered in pigeon-droppings? Those swaggering[14] birds are everywhere. Dog is delighted. He chases them around, barking and leaping[15] with joy.

3 They come to a row of shops, and the windows are 35 stuffed with desirable items. Minute mobilfons[16], packed with advanced features, everything compact and cleverly made; movie cameras small enough to fit in your hand; cunning[17] miniature music items, a thousand different types, more, at your command; wall-sized televi- 40 sions with pictures of amazing vividness, imagine sitting back with a glass of beer to watch the football, better than being at the match, better view; programmable CD players; multi-function DVD players; high-

---

[1] **Zaporozhets 965** a series of supermini city cars produced in Soviet Ukraine from 1958 to 1994; the cars had the nickname "Hunchback" (*Buckel*) because of their shape – [2] **humpbacked** *buckling, höckrig* – [3] **fibreboard** *Holzfaserplatte* – [4] **Trabant** a car produced in the former German Democratic Republic from 1957–1990, made of Duroplast, a kind of plastic – [5] **bonnet** *Motorhaube* – [6] **to tinker** *herumbasteln, werkeln* – [7] **drain** *Abwasserkanal* – [8] **miscellaneous** [ˌmɪsəlˈeɪnɪəs] consisting of a mixture of various things/smells – [9] **Angliski** (*Ukrainian*) English, in English – [10] **sheer** *bloß, rein* – [11] **battered** damaged, esp. by being used a lot – [12] **smoke-belcher** a car that ejects a lot of bad-smelling exhaust fumes – [13] **to blot sth. out** *etw. verdunkeln, abdecken* – [14] **to swagger** *stolzieren* – [15] **to leap** (leapt, leapt) to make a large jump – [16] **minute mobilfon** a very compact mobile phone – [17] **cunning** (*old use*) pretty and attractive

45 spec computers with unimaginable numbers of rams, gigs, hertz, etc. Too much choice. Yes, so many things that you didn't even know they existed to be desired.

He lingers, he reads the lists of social features, studies them almost furtively[18], as if standing on the threshold 50 of uncharted[19] sin. Such a surfeit[20] of everything. Where did all this stuff come from? Irina is trailing behind, staring into the window of a clothes shop, a look of un-belief on her face.

Food shops, restaurants – everything is here, yes, every 55 corner of the globe has been rifled[21] to furnish this abundance[22]. And the people, too, have been rifled from all over – Europe, Africa, India, the Orient, the Ameri-cas, so many different types all mixed together, such a crowd from everywhere under the sun, rubbing shoul-60 ders on the pavements without even looking at each other. Some are talking on mobilfons – even the women. And all well dressed – clothes like new. And the shoes – new shoes made of leather. No carpet slippers[23], like people wear in the street back home.

65 "Watch out!"

4 He is so intent on the shoes that he almost stumbles into a young woman walking fast-fast on high heels, who backs away snarling[24], "Get off me!"

"What are you dreaming about, Andriy?"

70 Irina grabs him and pulls him out of the way. The feel of her hand on his arm is like quickfire[25]. The woman walks on even faster. The look in her eyes – it was worse than contempt[26]. She looked straight through him. He didn't register in her eyes at all. His clothes – his best shirt 75 shabby and washed out, brown trousers that were new when he left home, Ukrainian trousers made of cheap fabric[27] that is already shapeless, held up by a cheap im-itation-leather belt, and imitation-leather shoes begin-ning to split at the toes – his clothes make him invisible.

80 "Everybody looks so smart. It makes me feel like a coun-try peasant[28]," says Irina, as if she can read his thoughts. This girl. Yes, her jeans are worn and strawberry stained, but they fit delightfully over her curves, and her hair gleams like a bird's wing and she's smiling teeth and 85 dimples[29] at all the world.

"Don't say that. You look …" He wants to put his arms round her. "… you look normal."

Should he put his arms round her? Better not – she might shriek "Leave me alone!" So they walk on, just wandering aimlessly through the streets, opening their 90 eyes to all there is to be seen. Dog runs ahead making a nuisance of himself, diving in between people's legs. Yes, this London – it's quite something.

But why – this is what he can't understand – why is there such abundance here, and such want back home? 95 For Ukrainians are as hard working as anybody – hard-er, because in the evenings after a day's work they grow their vegetables, mend[30] their cars, chop[31] their wood. You can spend your whole life toiling, in Ukraine, and still have nothing. You can spend your whole life toil-100 ing[32], and end up dead in a hole in the ground, covered with fallen coal. Poor Dad.

"Look!"

5 Irina is pointing to a small dark-skinned woman wearing a coloured scarf like the women of the former 105 eastern republics. She has a baby bundled up in her arms, and she is approaching passers-by, begging for money. The baby is horribly deformed, with a harelip[33] and one eye only partially opened.

"Have you got any money, Andriy?" 110

He fumbles in his pockets, feeling vaguely annoyed[34] with the woman, because he hasn't much money left, and would rather spend it on … well, not on her, any-way. But he sees the way Irina is looking at the baby.

"Take it please," he says in Ukrainian, handing her two 115 pound coins. The woman looks at the coins, and at them, and shakes her head.

"Keep your money," she says in broken Russian. "I have more than you."

She takes the baby off and sidles up[35] to a Japanese cou-120 ple who are photographing a statue covered with pi-geon-droppings.

They have already turned and started to retrace their steps when Irina spots, in the window of a stylish res-taurant where the tables are set for the evening meal, a 125 small card discreetly stuck in one corner *Staff wanted. Good pay. Accommodation[36] provided.*

"Oh, Andriy! Look! This may be just the right place for us. Here in the heart of London. Let's enquire[37]." […]

from *Two Caravans* by Marina Lewycka. Penguin, London, 2012, pp. 203 ff.

---

[18] **furtively** secretly and often dishonestly – [19] **uncharted** completely new – [20] **surfeit** more than is needed – [21] **to rifle** to search quickly through sth. – [22] **abundance** *Überfluss* – [23] **carpet slipper** *Stoffschuhe aus (alten) Teppichen* – [24] **to snarl** a deep, rough sound, usually made in anger – [25] **quickfire** *Schnellfeuer; wie aus der Pistole geschossen* – [26] **contempt** *Verachtung* – [27] **fabric** *Textil* – [28] **peasant** ['pɛznt] a member of a low social class of farm workers and owners of small farms – [29] **dimple** *Grübchen* – [30] **to mend sth.** to repair sth. – [31] **to chop** *hacken* – [32] **to toil** to work very hard – [33] **harelip** *Lippenspalte* – [34] **annoyed** angry and upset – [35] **to sidle up** to walk towards or away from sb, trying not be noticed – [36] **accommodation** a place to live, work and stay in – [37] **to enquire about sth.** to ask for information

COMPREHENSION

Andriy and Irina are seasonal workers from Ukraine, who work as pickers on a strawberry farm in England. On the farm, they live in caravans the farmer has put up at the workers' disposal. On a day off, they are visiting London for the first time. The excerpt from the novel at hand depicts their experiences and impressions.

1. Work with the text in a paired reading activity:
   a) Read the excerpt from the novel on your own first.
   b) After each paragraph, summarize the most relevant information to each other. Clarify possible questions/vocabulary, and correct and/or add information that you consider to be important.
   c) Find an appropriate headline for each of the paragraphs.

2. Find examples in the text that reveal Andriy's feelings for Irina.

3. While following Andriy and Irina walking through London, the reader gets a lot of information about the social, economic and cultural differences between London and Ukraine and its inhabitants. Find these differences in the text and complete the grid provided on worksheet 16.1.

SNG-40217-016
Worksheet 16.1

   Tip: Some of the differences refer to different categories, e. g. economic and social.

4. Collect examples from the text that serve as markers of social and cultural identity.

ANALYSIS

5. Examine the use and function of direct and indirect characterization* employed in the text.
   → Prep Course *kompakt*, Characterization of a Figure in Literature, p. 34

6. Interpret the setting (London) and its symbolic meaning.

7. Identify the narrative perspective* and give examples of the narrator's view of London.
   → Appendix, Literary Terms, p. 135

Info

- In a **direct characterization of a character** the narrator (or one of the other characters) directly **tells** the reader what the character's personality is.
- In an **indirect characterization** the writer **shows** the character talking and acting, and thus reveals the character's personality.
   a) **Speech** (what and how does the character communicate?)
   b) **Thoughts** (in a monologue, diary entry, etc.)
   c) **Actions** (how does the character behave?)
   d) **Looks** (appearance, body language, gestures, etc.)

ACTIVITIES

8. *After the exciting day in London, Andriy and Irina …*
   Write a continuation of the excerpt and think about what the two protagonists might experience or do next.

Step 1:
Team up with a partner and develop ideas on further events that might happen.

Tip: Irina and Andriy …
- enter the "stylish restaurant" and apply for the job.
- suddenly find out that a pickpocket has stolen their money … papers …
- return to the strawberry farm and tell the other migrant workers about their trip to London. Then …

Step 2:

Think about possible complications that might occur in order to flesh out your story and make it more exciting, e. g.

- the trouble Irina and Andriy might run into in the "stylish restaurant" because of their appearance and/or ethnic background,
- Irina and Andriy are offered a job in the restaurant as … , but the owner wants them to …,
- there has been a robbery/shoplifting incident in Oxford Street and Irina and Andriy get mistakenly arrested …

Step 3:

Before you start working out and writing a scene, think about its possible structure, and roughly sketch out the possible plot. You can use worksheet 16.2 for your ideas and notes.

Step 4:

Note that the creative writing task requires you to imagine what the characters introduced in the excerpt might do or say and put yourself in their position. Accordingly, you have to adapt to the characters' way of thinking, speaking or (re-)acting as shown in the text.

Examples:

- Andriy often compares his Ukrainian home to the situation in England:
    → *Back home in Kiev, restaurants are way more …*
- Andriy feels inferior because of his appearance.
    → *I wish my clothes would look better so that …*
- Irina dreams of living in London.
    → *Andriy, London is so much better than this horrible strawberry farm and caravans …*
- Irina's English is better than Andriy's.
    → *Andriy, let me speak to the boss of the restaurant first …*

Step 5:

Now, write a continuation of the excerpt at hand.

Tip: Be careful to follow the structural pattern of the scene at hand.

- Combine dialogue/monologue and descriptions/explanations/comments.
- You might use different type faces, e. g. bold print (*Fettdruck*), italics (*Kursivschrift*), capitalization (*Großbuchstaben*).
- Your text may have a funny, surprising, tragicomic or sad and melancholic ending.
- → Prep Course *kompakt*, Continuation of a Fictional Text, p. 46

GRAMMAR / LANGUAGE >>>>>>>>

9. Irina is already making plans for the future whereas Andriy is still caught in his Ukrainian past and always compares it to his life in England. Use different types of **conditional clauses (if-clauses) and comparisons** that reflect their thoughts about what

a) went wrong in the past/was different in Ukraine.

b) could be done in the future to improve their situation.

Examples:

- If my family hadn't been so extremely poor, I would not have been forced to … (type III)
- If we can get the job in the stylish restaurant, we will be able to … (type II)
- In Ukraine, people are much more sociable and helpful than in England … (comparison of adjectives)

→ Appendix, Conditional Sentences (If-Clauses), p. 119
→ Appendix, Adjectives and Adverbs, p. 115

SNG-40217-016 @
Worksheet 16.2

The Nearer the Friends, the Stronger the Regional Identity

AWARENESS

Travelling, going abroad, learning about new people and countries …
What do you think about it? Are you a homebody or have you caught the travel bug? Discuss in class.

A new job, an academic career or a romantic relationship – there are many reasons for young people to move. But this does not necessarily lead to happiness. Satisfaction increases when people can identify with the region
5 in which they live. The proximity of people who are emotionally important to them, however, is essential for creating this feeling of commitment[1]. Psychologists at Friedrich Schiller University, Jena, have now identified and described these factors and their effects in a longi-
10 tudinal[2] study. They have reported their research findings in the top tier[3] journal *Developmental Psychology*. "As well as professional and personal success, it is mostly a person's commitment to his place of residence that is decisive for a truly successful life," explains Dr
15 Elisabeth Borschel, who carried out the study as part of her doctoral research. "However, young adults in particular are under enormous pressure to be mobile, as they are expected to move frequently in order to make a start in life. We have studied the resulting tensions[4]
20 more closely in a longitudinal study. The study was funded by the Free State of Thuringia[5]."

Skyping is no substitute for personal proximity[6]
The Jena psychologists studied more than 1,000 students throughout Germany shortly before they graduated and
25 then on two more occasions within the next year. Five hundred of them left the place where they had studied, while a second group did not move. The researchers also recorded the places of residence[7] of the people named by the students as being important to them – family mem-
30 bers, friends or partners. The panel study[8] showed that the proximity of such key social contacts was of great influence on the way people identified with the region they lived in. "This is a surprising and therefore very enlightening result for us, as it contradicts[9] a major
35 promise of post-modern society and capitalism, which is

that in our era of high mobility and modern means of communication, we can also maintain relationships independently of time and space," says Prof. Franz J. Neyer of the University of Jena, who also worked on the study. "It would seem that Skype or e-mails cannot compensate 40 for the loss of personal – and thus geographical – proximity." This means that the greater the distance, the greater the dissatisfaction.

Moving away also has an impact on those who remain 45
Admittedly, there are also interactions between the emergence[10] of a regional identity and the creation of a social network. "It really is a two-edged sword," says Elisabeth Borschel, "because someone who identifies with his geographical surroundings also finds it easier to 50 establish important social contacts. For this reason, mobility cannot be condemned[11] in principle[12], but the new location has to meet the right basic conditions for a person to find new people he or she can relate to." Employers, for example, should take this into account[13] and sup- 55 port it when they advertise for new recruits nationwide. "In addition, we can identify what is called passive mobility," says Neyer. "This means that if a person moves away, it also affects the significant people who stay behind – the identification with their surroundings also 60 fades[14]." Therefore, the research results should be taken into account in political decisions, because the spatial[15] proximity between significant contacts also has effects on the state of a society. Appropriate[16] measures which do not force young people to move to a new location to 65 find a job – economic structural support[17], for example – could be a means of significantly[18] boosting[19] the satisfaction of people living in this region.

Friedrich-Schiller-Universität Jena, https://www.sciencedaily.com/releases/2019/03/190312103705.htm, 12 March 2019 [20.07.2019]

---

[1] **commitment** *Bindung* – [2] **longitudinal** longitudinal research is done on people or groups over a period of time – [3] **tier** [tɪər] one of several layers or levels – [4] **tension** a feeling of nervousness or anger – [5] **Free State of Thuringia** *Freistaat Thüringen* – [6] **proximity** *(fml.)* closeness – [7] **place of residence** *Wohnort* – [8] **panel study** *Längsschnittuntersuchung* – [9] **to contradict** *widersprechen* – [10] **emergence** the fact of sth. becoming known or starting to exist – [11] **to condemn** *verdammen* – [12] **in principle** *grundsätzlich* – [13] **to take sth. into account** *(idm.) etw. in Betracht ziehen* – [14] **to fade** to lose strength gradually – [15] **spatial** *räumlich* – [16] **appropriate** *angemessen* – [17] **economic structural support** money given by the government – [18] **significant** important or noticeable – [19] **to boost** to improve or increase sth.

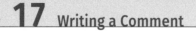
1. After reading the text, complete the following sentence with evidence from the text:
Skyping is no substitute for personal proximity because …

SNG-40217-017
Worksheet 17.1 @ **2.** Get a more detailed understanding of the academic findings and do the tasks provided on worksheet 17.1.

3. Juxtapose (*gegenüberstellen*) and contrast the results of the study in the categories 'happiness/satisfaction' and 'unhappiness/dissatisfaction'.

Team up with a partner and complete the grid below.

happiness/satisfaction	unhappiness/dissatisfaction
● identification with the region	● being expected to move frequently
● …	● …

→ Prep Course *kompakt*, Analysis of a Non-Fictional Text, p. 22

4. **Write a comment in response to the article in which you critically state whether (or not) you agree with the Thuringian academic study results and the conclusions they draw from them.**

Tip: A comment falls into the category of non-fictional texts. Its argumentative character aims at influencing the reader directly and requires a clear structure and the use of rhetorical devices.
a) Reactivate your knowledge of **forms of argumentative texts**.
    → Prep Course *kompakt*, Basic Types of Non-Fictional Texts, p. 8
b) The skills page "Writing a Comment" will help you to structure your text.
    → Prep Course *kompakt*, Writing a Comment and a Review, p. 52

Step 1:
Think about a concise and strong introduction, in which you raise a controversial question or refer to a disputed example or event. You can also make an (provocative) introductory remark or statement on a disputed matter.

Examples:
● Home is not a place, it's people.
● Home is where the heart is.
● There is no place like home.
● Strangers are just friends waiting to happen.

Step 2:
In the main part of your comment, state and describe the pros and cons of your topic.

Tip: Do not just state your opinions, but collect valid arguments and examples that support your view. If you are not sure about the matter, do further research and find events, quotations, etc. that serve as examples.

Step 3:

Decide on the structure of your argumentation:
- listing structure,
- progressive structure or
- antithetical structure

and sort your material accordingly.

→ Prep Course *kompakt*, Basic Types of Non-Fictional Texts, p. 8

Tip: Use the general pattern of **introduction – main part – conclusion** for your comment.
- **introduction** (answering the w-questions who – what – where – when – why? and attracting the reader's attention)
- **main part** (presenting arguments)
- **conclusion** (briefly summarizing the main ideas)

Tips on vocab ⫸

> I consider that ▪ I believe that ▪ I hold the view that ▪ To my mind ▪ I have the impression that ▪ As far as I know ▪ I am sure about/of ▪ I have doubts about ▪ I doubt that ▪ It seems possible that ▪ It's rather unlikely ▪ The author seems to ▪ I (dis-)agree with ▪ The author has reason to believe ▪ I share/don't share the author's view on ▪ I consider it be right/wrong to say ▪ I would like to clarify ▪ The author's opinion/ statement contrasts with/contradicts

Tip: Use connectives and linking phrases to make your text more fluent.

Tips on vocab ⫸

> furthermore ▪ for example ▪ yet ▪ however ▪ as well as ▪ perhaps ▪ because of this ▪ having said that ▪ on the contrary ▪ beyond that ▪ moreover ▪ in order to ▪ despite ▪ bearing in mind ▪ on the other hand

Step 4:

Write the comment in a coherent text of about 300 words, and express your views on the matter.

Tip: Remember to refer to the text and employ quotes to substantiate your arguments.

→ Prep Course *kompakt*, Writing a Comment and a Review, p. 52

GRAMMAR / LANGUAGE ⫸⫸⫸⫸

5. Reactivate and boost your vocabulary, finding **synonyms and/or antonyms** (= a word that means the opposite) to the words and phrases taken from the text.

   SNG-40217-017 @
   Worksheet 17.2   Complete the grid provided on worksheet 17.2.

Johnson

Mother Tongues

AWARENESS ▶▶▶▶▶

Step 1:

You have been learning at least one foreign language so far.

- What did/do you like/dislike about learning it?
- Have you learned something about the foreign culture in addition to the language as well? If so – what?

Step 2:

Louis D. Brandeis (1856 – 1941) born in the USA himself, was a son of Jewish immigrant parents from what today is the Czech Republic.

Jhumpa Lahiri (*1967) is an American author of Indian descent, the daughter of Bengali Indian parents.

Looking at the statements below, what do both express about the cultural and social impact of giving up one's mother tongue?

> What is Americanization? It manifests[1] itself, in a superficial way, when the immigrant adopts the clothes, the manners and the customs generally prevailing[2] here. Far more important is the manifestation presented when he substitutes for his mother tongue the English language as the common medium of speech.   *Louis D. Brandeis*
>
> I don't know Bengali perfectly. I don't know how to write it or even read it. I have an accent, I speak without authority[3], and so I've always perceived[4] a disjunction[5] between it and me. As a result, I consider my mother tongue, paradoxically, a foreign language.   *Jhumpa Lahiri*

1 Forcing immigrants to learn English can be counter-productive

Lev Golinkin left Soviet Ukraine as a nine-year-old in 1990. With assistance from HIAS[6], a Jewish organisa-
5 tion that helps refugees, his family made its way to Indiana. In America, not having English felt "like having a massive stroke[7], only instead of being sent to the hospital and getting help you have to go out and get a job." His experience suggests immigrants don't have to be
10 told how important it is to speak the language of a new country: they are more painfully aware of it than natives can ever know.

2 Yet they are often assumed[8] to need coercion[9]. On March 16th, for example, Donald Trump vowed to en-
15 sure that immigrants to America learn English and pass a civics exam[10] before arriving.

Such strictures[11] might seem to serve national cohesion[12]. In fact, the wrong policies and tone do the reverse[13], as Vicky Fouka of Stanford University found in a study of German-Americans living a century ago. 20 With its large German-immigrant population, Ohio was the first of several states to permit teaching in German alongside English. By 1900 some 4% of elementary-school pupils in America were taught at least partly in German. After the first world war anti-German senti- 25 ment[14] led to the end of those programmes and, in Ohio and Indiana, even to a ban on teaching German as a foreign language to children.

Ms Fouka compared German-American populations in border counties of Ohio and Indiana with their neigh- 30 bours in adjacent[15] states (who experienced no language ban). She found that those affected by the ban

---

[1] **to manifest sth.** (*fml.*) to show sth. clearly – [2] **to prevail** (*fml.*) to get control or influence – [3] **authority** here: expert – [4] **to perceive sth.** to have a belief about sth. – [5] **disjunction** (*fml.*) a difference or lack of connection between two things – [6] **HIAS** (*abbr.*) founded as the Hebrew Immigrant Aid Society in 1881, HIAS helped Jews fleeing progroms; today helps refugees and migrants worldwide – [7] **stroke** *Schlag* – [8] **to assume sth.** *etw. vermuten* – [9] **coercion** (*fml.*) *Nötigung, Zwang* – [10] **civics exam** *Prüfung in Staatsbürgerkunde* – [11] **stricture** (*fml.*) a statement of severe criticism – [12] **cohesion** [kəʊˈhiːʒən] *Zusammenhalt* – [13] **reverse** the opposite – [14] **sentiment** (*fml.*) *Empfindung* – [15] **adjacent** [əˈdʒeɪsənt] (*fml.*) very near, next to

were more likely to marry another German and give their children German names, and less likely to enlist[16]
35 during the second world war. Forced assimilation backfired[17] at every level, from the personal to the political.

[3] Unless the intention was not assimilation at all. Sometimes language laws are mostly symbolic. For in-
40 stance, numerous American states have declared English to be their official tongue (at a federal level, the country doesn't have one). This seems intended to send a message – "We speak English here" – without doing much to change reality on the ground. Sometimes,
45 though, laws seem designed to make life as hard as possible for immigrants.

[4] Take proposition 227 of 1998, whereby Californian voters eliminated almost all of the state's bilingual[18] education programmes. Bilingual teaching was always
50 intended as a bridge to English, but in a polarising[19] campaign it was portrayed as allowing kids to avoid[20] English altogether. (A few years earlier, another vote had stripped[21] illegal immigrants of state benefits.) A later analysis provided scant[22] evidence[23] that Proposi-
55 tion 227 made much difference to English-learning. But the Republican-led anti-immigration backlash of the 1990s led to a counter-backlash[24]: California Latinos, though often religious and socially conservative, have been solidly Democratic since.
60 California's conservatives were right to spot a rising cohort[25] of foreign-born residents. They had two options: to try to make them patriotic Americans (and Republi-

can voters) with a positive appeal, or to threaten[26] them with punishments. Choosing the latter, they lost twice, in both language and politics.
65

Californians overwhelmingly repealed[27] Proposition 227 in 2016. The state is riotously[28] multilingual, even as English remains the essential language, as it is in the rest of the country.

[5] Just how permissive[29] should receiving countries[30] 70 be? Corine Dehabey, a Syrian-American, who helps immigrants learn English in today's Ohio, thinks that, if policies are too accommodating[31], there is a risk that people don't feel any pressure to acquire[32] the language. But if she could make one change, it would be to give 75 them more time to do so. Current policies push newcomers to find work as soon as possible. That leads to doctors and engineers driving taxis, because they have yet to requalify in America.

Adults often struggle to learn a new language, as Mr 80 Golinkin's mother did, going from being a psychiatrist[33] in Ukraine to a security guard in America.

Some pull it off[34], as Mr Golinkin's father did by studying English for years before the move. But nearly all children master their adopted country's language, as Mr 85 Golinkin (now a writer) did quickly.

Children are sponges[35] for languages – and for attitudes, too. Their views of their new homes will forever be shaped by the way they are treated when they arrive.

The Economist, 25 May 2019, p. 78 (Republished with permission of The Economist, from The Economist, 25 May 2019, permission conveyed through Copyright Clearance Center, Inc.)

COMPREHENSION »»»»»

 1. In a paired reading activity, team up with a partner.

Step 1:
- In a **first reading**, **scan** the text section by section individually.
- Clarify unknown vocabulary and questions.
- Summarize the respective section to your partner and try to find an appropriate headline that reflects its content.

Step 2:
Together with your partner, go through the text section by section **a second time**, now **focusing on details** and take notes on the following aspects:

---

[16] **to enlist** to join the armed forces – [17] **to backfire** to have the opposite effect from the one intended – [18] **bilingual** [baɪˈlɪŋgwəl] able to use two languages equally well – [19] **to polarise** to cause something that divides people into completely opposing groups – [20] **to avoid** *vermeiden* – [21] **to strip sb. of sth.** (*phr. v.*) to take sth. important away from sb. as a punishment – [22] **scant** very little and not enough – [23] **evidence** *Beweise* – [24] **backlash** a strong negative reaction to sth. – [25] **cohort** a group of people who share a characteristic – [26] **threaten** *(be-)drohen* – [27] **to repeal** to remove the legal force of a law – [28] **riotously** [ˈraɪˌətəsli] in a very loud and uncontrolled way – [29] **permissive** tolerant – [30] **receiving country** the country that takes in the refugees/immigrants – [31] **accommodating** eager and willing to give what is needed to sb. – [32] **to acquire** here: to learn – [33] **psychiatrist** [saɪˈkaɪətrɪst] *Psychiater* – [34] **to pull sth. off** (*infml.*) to succeed, *etw. durchziehen* – [35] **sponge** [spʌndʒ] *Schwamm*

1
- Lev Golinkin's experiences with English
- the need to learn the language of the new country

2
- Donald Trump's idea of a civics exam
- Vicky Fouka's study of German-Americans in Ohio and Indiana
- the effects of banning teaching German in school

3
- the intention behind declaring English as the official language

4
- bilingual education programmes in California and their elimination
- the impact of Proposition 227 of 1998
- the Californians' reaction to Proposition 227 in 2016

5
- Ohio's immigrant policy today and its consequences
- Mr Golinkin's and his father's way of coping with English as a foreign language

ANALYSIS

2. Examine the author's line of argument* and explain how it supports the message of the text.
→ Prep Course *kompakt*, Analysis of a Non-Fictional Text, p. 22

3. Analyse how the author's use of positive and negative emotive words emphasizes his stance on forcing immigrants to adapt and to learn the new country's language.

ACTIVITIES

4. Write a *Letter to the Editor* on the controversial topic, expressing your personal view on whether (or not) immigrants should be forced to learn English, and as a consequence, abandon their mother tongue and their inherited culture.

Tip: Although you should generally aim at expressing your thoughts straightforwardly and frankly, try to use a more neutral language register and avoid being too informal so as not to appear judgmental or biased. Use your dictionary to find appropriate words and double-check certain formulations if you are not sure about them.

Step 1:
Reactivate your knowledge about how to write a **formal letter** (or e-mail).
→ Prep Course *kompakt*, Writing a Formal Letter, p. 54

Step 2:
If necessary, do further research on the matter in order to have further examples.

Example:
I read your comprehensive article published in *The Economist* on 25 May 2019 with great interest …
Your article considers the problems connected with immigration … However, I would like to …

Tip: In order to approach the issue fairly, try to show an understanding of both sets of views while still expressing your view on the topic clearly and in a balanced and factual way.

Tips on vocab »»»
- I was really surprised to find out that …
- I read a fascinating article about …
- What would it be like if …?
- It is absolutely astonishing to see that …
- From my own perspective …

Step 3:

Structure the body of your letter clearly and avoid unnecessary repetition. Include examples, arguments and references to support your point of view.

Step 4:

Conclude your letter with a summarizing sentence and an outlook on the issue, e. g. by asking a (rhetorical) question or making a suggestion on possible alternatives.

→ Appendix, Connectives and Adverbs, p. 120

→ Prep Course *kompakt*, Writing a Letter to the Editor, p. 56

→ Prep Course *kompakt*, Conversation and Discussion, p. 38

Example:

I would like to conclude my letter by expressing my general understanding of the state's/government's wish to … However, if academic research and history teach us … As can be seen in many examples, if people are senselessly forced into doing something the necessity of which they do not understand, they …

GRAMMAR / LANGUAGE ▶▶▶▶▶▶

5. Use the information given in the magazine article and formulate **conditional sentences (if-clauses) of different types** in order to express
   a) what could have been done in Ohio and Indiana to avoid the backfiring of assimilation.
   b) what Californian conservatives should have done differently.
   c) what made Lev Golinkin study English (quickly).
   d) the author's (implied) demands concerning how to treat immigrants.

   Examples:
   - If bilingual teaching in Indiana/Ohio schools hadn't been abolished, they wouldn't have … (type III)
   - If immigrants don't learn the new country's language properly, they will not … (type I)
   → Appendix, Conditional Sentences (If-Clauses), p. 119

6. Imagine the government set up a set of guidelines and recommendations on how to handle the language acquisition of immigrants.
   Set up these guidelines and employ **gerund and participle constructions** to improve your style and increase the fluency of your writing.

   Examples:
   - Welcoming and showing understanding to people who have escaped … and are trying to find a new home is …
   - As everybody knows, giving positive incentives and motivating people to … is more important than …
   → Appendix, Participle, p. 127
   → Appendix, Infinitive With/Without 'to' and the Gerund, p. 124

 7. The article is predominantly written in formal English. Turn the words and phrases provided on worksheet 18.1 into everyday English and use a dictionary for help where necessary.

 8. Worksheet 18.1 provides you with further sentences from the magazine article. Turn these sentences into the **passive voice** to make the formulations less personal.
   → Appendix, Passive, p. 128

5 Units – 5 Topics – 5 Articles

After having worked with various units, topics and material provided in the *Prep Course*, you will have gained a lot of knowledge and skills to do a project that applies all these aspects.

A newspaper front page or template as well as an example of a front page from the British quality newspaper *The Guardian* give you an overview of the core elements of a front page.

The **front cover** of an issue of the British daily newspaper *The Guardian*, published on 9 May 2019

A so-called **template** (= a particular model for arranging information or images in a document, etc. that you can copy and use for your own purposes) of a typical newspaper front page illustrating the various elements

1. Form five teams of students, one team for each unit/topic of the *Prep Course*.
   Discuss and decide in class whether each of the five teams compiles one complete front page or whether you distribute the space available on one front page among the whole class so that each group completes one fifth of the page.

Step 1:
You can use the texts and material provided in the *Prep Course*, and/or do further research on your chosen topic, decide what kind of article you are going to write and which further material (photos, infographics, further texts, etc.) you will need.

Step 2:
Reactivate your knowledge of the characteristics of newspapers and what to consider when writing a newspaper article.
Additionally, you can use the information given in the check list below and in the template on the opposite page.
→ Prep Course *kompakt*, The Press, p. 10
→ Prep Course *kompakt*, Writing a Newspaper Article, p. 58

2. Write your newspaper article(s) and arrange them on the front page of your newspaper.

   Tip: You should use a computer to typeset your articles and (roughly) plan the arrangement of the various elements you want to use.

3. Display your front page(s) in class and compare, discuss and evaluate the various articles, further materials, etc.

Checklist

elements ...	... function ...
● masthead	→ newspaper's name printed in special type
● lead (paragraph)	→ usually set in bold (*Fettdruck*), italics (*Kursivschrift*) or larger text
● columns of writing	→ articles, reports, etc.
● by-line	→ journalist's name and job title
● cut	→ photo or illustration
● index	→ alphabetized table of contents of the newspaper
● photo credit	→ reference to the source of a photograph or illustration
● banner (streamer)	→ headline that runs across the full page, used for important news or scandals
● classifieds	→ advertisements in small type, often submitted by individuals or small traders
● editorial (leader)	→ article that represents the newspaper's opinion
● subhead	→ one- or two-lined headline at the head of a paragraph to structure the text
● anchor	→ light-hearted, human interest story placed at the bottom of front page

Appendix

Grammar and Language

Supplementary Booklet

Prep Course *kompakt* – Skills & Competences

Adjectives and Adverbs

Adjectives

Adjectives describe the quality of a noun; an adjective tells what sth./sb. is like.

The regular comparison with 'er' and 'est'

Monosyllabic (= one syllable) and disyllabic (= two syllables) adjectives with the endings '-er', '-le', '-ow' and '-y':

comparative and superlative forms	examples		
→ monosyllabic adjectives:	old	older	the oldest
	low	lower	the lowest
	thin	thinner	the thinnest
	high	higher	the highest
	large	larger	the largest
→ disyllabic adjectives:	happy	happier	the happiest
	easy	easier	the easiest
	narrow	narrower	the narrowest
	simple	simpler*	simplest*
	*can also be used in the comparative form with "more"/"most"		

The irregular comparison with 'more' and 'most'

Disyllabic adjectives (= two syllables), trisyllabic (= three syllables) and polysyllabic (= many syllables) adjectives with endings **other than** '-er', '-le', '-ow' and '-y':

comparative and superlative forms	examples		
→ disyllabic, trisyllabic and polysyllabic adjectives:	useful	more useful	the most useful
	modern	more modern	the most modern
	beautiful	more beautiful	the most beautiful
	interesting	more interesting	the most interesting

The irregular comparison

⚠ Pay attention to the irregular forms:	good	better	the best
	bad	worse	the worst
	much	more	the most
	many	more	the most
	little *(klein)*	smaller	the smallest
	little *(wenig)*	less	the least
	far	further	the furthest
	late	later	the latest *(zeitlich)*
	late	latter	the latter *(Reihenfolge)*

Sentences with comparisons

- Linda is (not) as clever as Tom. → *(nicht) so … wie …*
- Susan is more excited than Lucy. → *mehr … als …*
- Michael is taller than Bill. → *mehr/größer … als …*
- The situation was getting worse and worse. → *schlechter und schlechter*
- The angrier the teacher got, the louder the students became. → *je … desto …*

Grammar and Language

Grammar and Language

Adverbs

An adverb quantifies or modifies (= *abwandeln, einschränken, relativieren*) the meaning of a verb, an adjective or a phrase/sentence.

Adverbs typically answer questions like how?/in what way? (**adverbs of manner**), when? (**adverbs of time**), how often? (**adverbs of frequency**), where? (**adverbs of place**), and to what extent? (**adverbs of degree**). This can be done by using a single word (e. g. slowly, suddenly, etc.) or by using an adverbial phrase or sentence (e. g. behind the wall, during the holidays, much too early, etc.).

There are **two different kinds of adverbs** in the English language:
a) adverbs that give information about time and place, e. g. here, there, now, then
b) adverbs that are formed from adjectives, e. g. nicely, beautifully, easily, by adding the ending '-ly' to the adjective.

The formation of adverbs

- attachment of '-ly': easy → easily; simple → simply; whole → wholly
- adjectives with an '-ly' ending: friendly → in a friendly way
- adjectives with an '-ic' ending: automatic → automatically
- adjectives and adverbs that have the same form and meaning: daily, hourly, weekly, monthly, yearly, early, likely, fast, long, far, straight, low

Adjectives that form adverbs with different meanings

adjective	adverb	adverb
right *(richtig)*	right *(richtig)*	rightly *(zurecht)*
hard *(hart)*	hard *(hart)*	hardly *(kaum)*
fair *(fair)*	fair *(fair)*	fairly *(ziemlich)*
deep *(tief)*	deep *(tief)*	deeply *(zutiefst)*
pretty *(hübsch)*	pretty *(ziemlich)*	prettily *(hübsch)*
high *(hoch)*	high *(hoch)*	highly *(höchst)*
late *(spät)*	late *(spät)*	lately *(in letzter Zeit)*
most *(am meisten)*	most *(am meisten)*	mostly *(meistens)*
short *(kurz)*	short *(kurz)*	shortly *(in Kürze)*

Comparison of adverbs

- adverbs that give information about time and place: attachment of '-er' and '-est'
  e. g. soon – sooner – the soonest; early – earlier – the earliest
- adverbs with an '-ly' ending: 'more' and 'most'
  e. g. easily – more easily – most easily

⚠ irregular forms of comparison		
adverb	**comparative**	**superlative**
well	better	best
much	more	most
little	less	least
badly/ill	worse	worst
near	nearer	nearest/next
far	further/farther	furthest/farthest
late	later	latest/last

The position of adverbs and adverbials in a sentence

- **adverbs of frequency** are usually put between the subject and main verb or between the auxiliary and main verb
  Owen always enjoyed the hard work in the quarry.
  Owen has always worked hard.
- **adverbs of manner** are usually put at the end of the sentence
  The student council had prepared the fall dance carefully.
- **adverbials of place/direction and time** can be placed at the end or at the beginning of the sentence depending on how much they are stressed
  Recently, Harold had learned how to play the banjo.
  In this neighbourhood, industrial sites have been threatening people's health for a long time.
- when there are **several adverbs and adverbials at the end of a sentence**, the rules are:
  - place/direction before time
    place   time
    Many students want to volunteer at a camp during the summer holidays.

  - adverbs of manner before place/direction and time
      manner place time
    Owen went slowly to the door last night.

  - precise time before general time
       place precise time general time
    Hester arrived at Owen's house at 8 o'clock last night.

Grammar and Language

British and American English

Though **Americanisms** are spreading rapidly worldwide, there are still a number of differences between American and British English. Here are some well-known examples of basic differences.

	British English	American English	
	British English	**American English**	
	pronunciation		
	– dance [dɑːns]	→ dance [dæns]	
	– water [ˈwɔːtə] *t* is spoken "*t*"	→ water [ˈwɑːtər] *t* is spoken "*d*"	
	– missile [ˈmɪsaɪl] -*ile* syllable is spoken "*ail*"	→ missile [ˈmɪsl] -*ile* syllable is spoken "*il*"	
	– art [aːt] "r" is not spoken	→ art [aːrt] "r" is spoken	
	spelling		
	– neighbour	→ neighbor	
	– offence	→ offense	
	– centre	→ center	
	– quarrelling, travelling	→ quarreling, traveling	
	– to organise	→ to organize	
	– catalogue	→ catalog	
	– programme	→ program	
	grammar		
	– Have you got …?	→ Do you have …?	
	– to get – got – got	→ to get – got – gotten	
	– to prove – proved – proved	→ to prove – proved – proven	
	– I have already written the letter. (present perfect)	→ I already wrote the letter. (simple past)	
	– He writes awfully. (adverb)	→ He writes awful. (adjective)	
	vocabulary		

BE	US	BE	US	BE	US
autumn	fall	dustbin	garbage can	pavement	sidewalk
note (money)	bill	filling station	gas station	petrol	gas
biscuit	cookie	film	movie	prison	jail/penitentiary
boot	trunk	flat	apartment	rubber	eraser
car park	parking lot	ground floor	first floor	shop	store
chemist's	drugstore	handbag	purse	sweets	candy
chips	French fries	lift	elevator	tap	faucet
company	corporation	lorry	truck	traffic light	stop light
cooker	stove	motorway	highway/freeway	trousers	pants
crisps	chips	number plate	license plate	underground	subway

Conditional Sentences (If-Clauses)

Conditional sentences are sentences that discuss **possible**, **almost impossible** or **impossible conditions** and their consequences. A conditional sentence has **two parts**: an if-clause (= the condition) and a main clause (= the consequence). There are **three types** of conditional sentences.

if-clause (condition)	main clause (consequence)
type I – possible conditions	
simple present	**will-future, modal auxiliary, imperative**
If the weather is nice, ...	we will go to the swimming pool.
If the weather is rainy, ...	we will not (won't) go for a walk.
If Hester does not behave at the ball, ...	she may get detention.
If you want to study abroad, ...	you can apply for a scholarship.
If you want to volunteer, ...	check the Internet for organizations first.
type II – almost impossible conditions	
simple past	**would + infinitive**
If Hester asked Owen for a date,	he would be very happy.
If I were you, ...	I would stop drinking so much alcohol.
If I had the opportunity to go abroad, ...	I would go right away.
type III – absolutely impossible conditions	
past perfect	**would + infinitive perfect**
If you had written the application on time, ...	they would have invited you for an interview.
If Hester had not drunk that much, ...	she would not have felt so sick the following day.
	would + infinitive
If you had not eaten all the chocolate, ...	you would not feel sick now.
	only used when the consequence is related to the present

 Generally, you **must not use will/would** in the if-clause when the **if-clause expresses a condition** (*Bedingung*).
If you do not pay the bill, you will be in trouble. (If you ~~will not pay~~ the bill, you will be …)

condition   consequence

You can use will/would in the if-clause when you are asking about **someone's willingness** to do something.
If you would help me, that would be wonderful …

Both **if** (*wenn, falls*) and **when** (*dann, wenn*) can be used to introduce if-clauses but they mean different things:
- use **if** if you are unsure whether you will do something or whether something will happen
  If I get a scholarship, I will take part in the exchange.
- use **when** if you are sure about doing something or if something will most likely happen
  When I get that scholarship, I will take part in the exchange.
- **if** can be used in all three types of conditional sentences, **when** is only used in type I-clauses.

Grammar and Language

Connectives and Adverbs

In order to improve your style and speak and write more fluently, you should employ connectives and adverbs. **Try to vary the beginnings of your sentences** and use sub-clauses to express your opinion and thoughts in a more diversified way.

listing/order first, second, third; firstly, secondly, thirdly; for one thing … (and) for another (thing); to begin with; to start with; initially/in the first place; then; finally; to conclude[1]; last but not least	**adding/reinforcing**[11] also; as well; too; furthermore; moreover; then; in addition to; above all; what is more; again; equally; generally speaking
comparison/similarity[2] equally; likewise; similarly; in the same way; compared to …; both; but while the first …; although; though	**summary/conclusion/consequence** then; all in all; to sum up; in conclusion; accordingly; as a result; briefly; consequently; generally speaking; hence; it follows that; taking everything into account; thus; therefore
exemplification[3] namely; for example (e. g.); for instance; that is (i. e.); that is to say	**reformulation** or rather; to put it another way; in other words
alternative alternatively; on the other hand	**contrast** on the contrary; in contrast; by contrast; on the one hand … on the other hand; compared to; although; likewise
concession[4] besides; however; nevertheless; still; though; in spite of that; on the other hand; despite this; admittedly[5]	**reason and purpose** as; because of; consequently; for this/that reason; hence; in order to; on account of; since; so; that explains why; this is why; therefore
emphasis[6] as a matter of fact; at any rate; clearly; evidently[7]; ideally; undoubtedly[8]	**condition** as long as; even if; if; in any case; on the condition that; provided that; unless
your own opinion from my point of view; in my opinion; in my view; the way I see it; to my mind; to my way of thinking	**an opposite point of view** alternatively; but; despite/in spite of (the fact); except for; however; in contrast to; instead of; nonetheless; on the contrary
reference[9] **to something/someone** according to; as for; the former; the latter; with reference to; referring to; with regard to; concerning	**assumption**[12] assuming that; given that; presumably; probably; granted that; allegedly[13]; seemingly; on the face of it; supposedly[14]
toning down[10] **arguments** a little (worrying); almost; fairly; hardly; more or less; somewhat; on second thought; at first sight	**emphasizing arguments** actually; absolutely; (not …) at all; badly (needed); completely; extremely; entirely; indeed; not in the least; perfectly; really; seriously; thoroughly; totally; utterly[15]; very

[1] **to conclude sth. from sth.** *schlussfolgern* – [2] **similarity** the state of being like sth./sb. but not exactly the same – [3] **exemplification** illustration, giving an example – [4] **concession** *Zugeständnis* – [5] **admittedly** accepting that sth. is true – [6] **to put emphasis on sth.** to stress sth. – [7] **evidently** clearly, obviously – [8] **undoubtedly** *zweifellos* – [9] **reference** sth. that you connect or relate to sth. else – [10] **to tone down sth.** to express an opinion in a less extreme or offensive way – [11] **to reinforce sth.** to make a feeling/an idea stronger – [12] **assumption** *Annahme, Vermutung* – [13] **allegedly** *angeblich* – [14] **supposedly** *angeblich, vermutlich* – [15] **utterly** totally, very much

English Word Pairs That Can Easily Be Mixed Up ⚠

to abuse – *missbrauchen*	**to misuse** – *missbrauchen, zweckentfremden*
to affect [əˈfekt] – *(ein)wirken auf*	**effect** [ɪˈfekt] – *Wirkung*
to borrow – *von jdm. etw. borgen*	**to lend** – *an jdn. etw. verleihen*
classic – *typisch, vorbildlich (klassisch)*	**classical** – *die Antike betreffend (klassisch)*
conscience [ˈkɒnʃəns] – *Gewissen*	**conscientious** [ˌkɒnʃiˈenʃes] – *gewissenhaft*
conscious [ˈkɒnʃəs] – *bewusst*	**consciousness** [ˈkɒnʃesnes] – *Bewusstsein*
economic – *(volks-)wirtschaftlich*	**economical** – *sparsam*
efficient – *tüchtig, leistungsfähig*	**effective** – *wirksam*
fat – *dick (Mensch, Profit, …)*	**thick** – *dick (Buch), dicht (Haar)*
first – *zuerst (als Erster …)*	**at first** – *zuerst (am Anfang)*
historic – *geschichtlich bedeutsam (historisch)*	**historical** – *historisch (Film, Buch) die Geschichte behandelnd*
industrial – *industriell*	**industrious** – *fleißig*
legible [ˈledʒabl] – *leserlich (Handschrift)*	**readable** [ˈriːdəbl] – *lesenswert*
literal – *wörtlich*	**literate** – *lesen und schreiben können, belesen/gebildet sein*
to loosen – *losmachen, lockern*	**to lose** – *verlieren*
policy – *Politik/Linie (einer Firma, Regierung)*	**politics** – *Politik (Staatskunst)*
practical – *praktisch (veranlagt), handlich*	**practicable** – *brauchbar, durchführbar*
presently – *bald, gleich*	**at present** – *im Augenblick, zurzeit*
principal – *Schulleiter(in) (US)*	**principle** – *Grundsatz*
to raise [reɪz] – *(an)heben, erhöhen*	**to rise** [raɪz] – *(auf)steigen (Sonne)*
receipt [rɪˈsiːt] – *Quittung*	**recipe** [ˈresəpi] – *Kochrezept*
self-confident – *selbstbewusst*	**self-conscious** – *befangen, gehemmt*
tasteful – *geschmackvoll*	**tasty** – *schmackhaft, lecker*
technique [tekˈniːk] – *Art der Ausführung, Technik (eines Künstlers)*	**technology** – *Technik, Technologie*

Grammar and Language

Indirect Speech

Usage

When you report what an author has written in a text or what a character says or thinks, it is necessary to use indirect speech.

In a summary, for example, you should *not* use direct speech *at all;* instead, use indirect speech. Write **an appropriate introductory sentence** and do not always use the verb "say" – vary your formulations.

Here are some alternative verbs for your introductory sentences:

Statements: to say, to tell, to comment (on), to add, to explain, to mention, to remark, to announce, to point out, to describe, to state, etc.

Questions: to ask, to want to know, to wonder whether/if, to doubt whether/if, etc.

Commands/requests: to tell (sb. to do sth.), to order, to demand, to request, etc.

Only (!) if the introductory verb is in the past tense, do you have to **backshift the tenses** of the direct speech.

backshift			example	
tenses			**direct speech**	**indirect speech**
present	→	past	"Owen works in the quarry in the holidays."	He said Owen worked in the quarry in the holidays.
past	→	past perfect	"Hester loved the boatman from Tortola."	Owen explained that Hester had loved the boatman from Tortola.
			"Hester was drinking all night."	Tom told us that Hester had been drinking all night.
present perfect	→	past perfect	"I have applied for the job."	Sally said that she had applied for the job.
will-future	→	would + infinitive	"I'm sure the new cars will be more energy-efficient."	The politician said that he was sure that the new cars would be more energy-efficient.
going to-future	→	was/were going to + infinitive	"The government is going to fight unemployment."	The President explained that the government was going to fight unemployment.
can	→	could	"I'm sorry we can't come."	Michael was sorry that they could not come.
may	→	might	"I may perform another fake suicide."	Harold mentioned that he might perform another fake suicide.

Indirect questions

- you also have to backshift the tenses in indirect questions
- there is **no do/does/did** in indirect questions
- the **sentence order** in indirect questions is the same as in statements: **s – v – o**
- if you report questions with question words like **who, what, where, when, why,** use **ask/want to know +** **question word**
- *Tom: "What did you write in the test?"*   → *Tom wanted to know what I had written in the test.*
- if there is no question word in the direct question, use **if** or **whether** in the indirect question
  Tom: "Do you love Hester, Owen?"   → *Tom wanted to know if Owen loved Hester.*

Indirect commands and requests

- are usually introduced with **tell sb. (not) to do sth., ask sb. (not) to do sth., warn sb. (not) to do sth.** or **remind sb. (not) to do sth.,** etc.
- usually require the **infinitive with to** or **not to**

	S	**V**	**O**	**infinitive**
"Don't drink so much." →	*The doctor*	*warned*	*him*	*not to drink* *so much.*
Susan: "Can you help me with the report?" →	*Susan*	*asked*	*me*	*to help* *her with the report.*

Changes of pronouns and adverbials of time and place

- **pronouns** and **adverbials of time and place** have to be adjusted to the perspective of the person reporting the statement and therefore might have to be changed

Hester: "Can I use your car, Owen?"   (Owen to his friend)
Hester asked me if she could use my car.
(Hester to her friend)
I asked Owen yesterday if I could use his car.

adverbials of time and place			
direct speech	**indirect speech**	**direct speech**	**indirect speech**
now →	then, at that time	last night/week/year →	the day/week/year before
today →	(on) that day, yesterday, on	three days ago →	three days before/earlier
	Monday …	this evening →	that evening
tomorrow →	the next day, the following	tonight →	that night
	day, today, …	here →	there
yesterday →	the day before		

- **further changes:** come → go,   bring → take,   this → that,   these → those

German *(zu-)lassen, machen lassen, veranlassen*

- **let + object + infinitive without to** → *(zu-) lassen, erlauben*
  In a multicultural society, it is important to let people keep the cultural traditions of their homeland.

- **permit/allow + object + infinitive with to** → *(zu-) lassen, erlauben*
  Some nations allow immigrants to have two nationalities.

- **have/get + object + past participle** → *machen lassen*
  Before Hester went to the ball, she had her hair done.
  When Pat prepared her project, she got some transparencies made in the copy shop.

- **have/make + object + infinitive without to** → *veranlassen, zwingen*
  The teacher had his students correct their own mistakes.
  The teacher cannot make the students work regularly.

- **get + object + infinitive with to** → *jdn. dazu bringen, zwingen*
  The United Nations should get the industrial nations to ban underpaid labour in sweat shops.

Infinitive With/Without 'to' and the Gerund

When two main verbs appear together, the second verb will take one of the following three forms:

1. The infinitive without 'to'

- the infinitive without 'to' is used **after modal verbs**, e. g. will, should, can, must, etc. and **certain verbs of permission and causation** (*Verursachung*), e. g. make, bid, let, and have (see above)
  He will study at Oxford next year.

2. The infinitive with 'to'

- the infinitive with 'to' is often used after verbs that can refer to **future actions**, e. g. afford, agree, appear, attempt, choose, dare, decide, expect, fail, help, hope, learn, manage, offer, plan, promise, refuse, seem, wish, would like, would love, would prefer, would hate
  The Hole in the Wall Camps help to give seriously ill children a wonderful vacation.
  I hope to work in a Hole in the Wall Camp next year.

3. The gerund

The gerund (formed with the **infinitive** (without 'to') + **-ing**) **is a special form of the verb** that is used like a noun.

- the **gerund** can be the subject of the sentence
  Travelling abroad is fun and broadens your horizons.

- the **gerund** can be the **object after certain verbs and phrases**, e. g. admit, avoid, consider, deny, hate, detest, dislike, love, like, enjoy, excuse, finish, imagine, keep (→ continue), (not) mind, miss, postpone, practise, prevent, regret, resist, resume, risk, stand (→ tolerate), suggest, cannot/could not help, it is no use, it is worth, look forward to
  Harold did not mind spending all his time with an old woman.

- the **gerund** is used **after prepositions**:
  a) **adjective + preposition**, e. g. capable of, famous for, fond of, good at, interested in, proud of
     Paul Newman became famous for playing Butch Cassidy in the famous Western.

  b) **noun + preposition**, e. g. difficulty in, fear of, hope of, intention of, a question of
     President Obama has the intention of motivating people to volunteer.

  c) **verb + preposition (= prepositional verbs)**, e. g. accuse sb. of, apologize for, believe in, count on, depend on, dream of, insist on, object to, prevent sth. from, rely on, succeed in, thank for
     Harold succeeded in shocking his mother by committing fake suicides.

 However, be careful with the word 'to'. It can function as a preposition.
We are very much looking forward to meeting you next week.

'To' can also be part of the infinitive with 'to' (see above).
They would like to meet us at the airport.

 The verbs like, love, hate, start, begin, continue, intend can be used with **a gerund** or **an infinitive with 'to'** with **little or no difference** in meaning.

In contrast, the verbs forget, go on, remember, stop, try have **a totally different meaning** when used with a gerund or infinitive.

Phil stopped eating a hamburger. → *Phil hörte auf, einen Hamburger zu essen.*
Phil stopped to eat a hamburger. → *Phil stoppte/hielt an, um einen Hamburger zu essen.*

Grammar and Language

The Language Register of English

Many English words and phrases have similar meanings, and are, at first sight, synonyms. However, different contexts or situations typically require more or less formal wording. Some synonyms are more appropriate or more commonly used in **formal texts or situations** (e. g. *to proceed*), whereas in more informal, **everyday spoken English**, you would choose another phrase (e. g. *to go ahead*). Formal or *Standard English* is written in formal documents, e. g. essays, business letters, (traditional) literature; it is spoken in business negotiations, news broadcasts, official examinations, etc.

Different registers of English

everyday English	formal English
• I'm sorry/Sorry/Pardon me/Excuse me …	→ I (would like to) apologize …
• In my opinion/view, … The way I see it, … (*spoken*) If you ask me, … (*spoken*)	→ I am of the opinion that … I take the view that … It is my belief that …
• Is it all right/OK if I … Do you think I could …	→ I was wondering whether I could … Would it bother you if I …?
• Why don't we …? Let's … How about …?/What about …?	→ Maybe we could …/Perhaps we could … You might like/want to … Shall we …?
• Hi! What's up? How are you? How are you doing?	→ How do you do? (formal, only used when meeting sb. for the first time) Pleased/Lovely/Nice to meet you.
• Thanks. I can't thank you enough.	→ I appreciate … I am most grateful …

Colloquialisms

Colloquial language (i. e. informal, relaxed speech) is only appropriate for casual, familiar or informal conversation and is **not used in formal speech or writing**, except for artistic purposes, such as in novels or poetry. Some examples are: *gonna* (going to), *wanna* (want to), *ain't nothin'* (there is not anything), *not the sharpest knife in the drawer* (not very smart/intelligent).

Slang

Slang words are used in **very informal** situations, and usually only by a specific social group, e. g. teenagers, soldiers, etc. or in literature and song texts. Typically, slang words or phrases are **taboo words** and are often meant in a derogatory way (i. e. insulting, disapproving). Here is an example taken from literature:

> I'm trying to sleep when the other cons on my row are waking up. One of them hears me sigh, and tosses some words through his door. "Little? You a fuckin star!"
> "Yeah, right," I say. "Tell the prosecution."
> "Hell, youse'll get the *bestest* fuckin attorneys, hear what I'm sayin?"
> "My attorney can't even speak fuckin English."
> "Nah," says the con, "they dissed his ass, he history. I saw on TV he said he still workin on it, but that's bullshit, he ain't even hired no more. You get big guns now, hear what I'm sayin?"
> from *Vernon God Little* by DBC Pierre, Faber and Faber, London 2003, pp. 197 f.

Grammar and Language

Modal Auxiliaries

Modal Auxiliaries with the Perfect Infinitive

Modal verbs or modal auxiliaries are a special group **of verbs that are different from other verbs** in **four ways**:

a) after modal auxiliaries the **infinitive** is used **without "to"**

b) modal auxiliaries have **no -s on the third-person singular**

c) **modal questions and negatives** are formed **without "to"**
   (*Can you help me?*, *You must not say that.*)

d) modal auxiliaries have **no infinitives** (~~to may~~) and **no participles** (~~caning, musted~~).
   Instead you use **substitute verbs**:

can	→	to be able to (*können*)
	→	to be allowed to (*dürfen*)
must	→	to have to (*müssen*)
may	→	to be allowed to (*dürfen*)
mustn't	→	not to be allowed to (*nicht dürfen*)
needn't	→	not to have to (*nicht müssen, nicht brauchen*)

- if you want to express that something **probably** happened in the past or that things might have been different in the past, you can use the modal auxiliaries **must, may, should, ought to, could, might, need (not)** with the perfect infinitive (**have + past participle**)
  Hester shouldn't have drunk so much.
  If you had told me, I could have helped you.
  I didn't hear the telephone. I must have been in the garden.

- in **German**, the construction of a modal auxiliary and the perfect infinitive is usually expressed as *Konjunktiv* (*hätte sollen, hätte müssen, etc.*)

Further modal auxiliaries:

- **should** is used to make a suggestion to sb./oneself
  I should eat more fruit.

- **have to** is used to talk about rules and laws
  You have to stop on red.

- **can**, **would**, **may** is used to ask for permission
  Can I borrow your bike? (everyday English)
  Could I ask a question? (polite, more formal English)
  May I have your name, please? (very formal English)

- **used to (+ infinitive)** is used for finished habits and situations (of the past)
  I used to have a red car. (Now I have a blue one) *Ich hatte (immer) ein rotes Auto …*

- **would like to** is used to talk about things that people want to do
  Would you like some lemonade?
  I would like to be taller.

Participle

Participle constructions instead of adverbial clauses

- you can use a present participle in place of an **adverbial clause of reason** (*Kausalsatz*)
  Tess travelled to the USA to learn English. → *Wanting to learn English, Tess travelled to the USA.*
  She failed her final exam because she did → *Having done too much sightseeing, she failed the final exam.*
  too much sightseeing.

- you can use a present participle in place of an **adverbial clause of time** (*Temporalsatz*)
  When Pat arrived in New York, she noticed → *Arriving in New York, Pat noticed that she had forgotten*
  she had forgotten her camera. *her camera.*

- you can use a present participle instead of an **adverbial clause of manner** (*Art und Weise, Modalsatz*)
  Phil spent all his pocket money in order to → *Phil spent all his pocket money buying the ticket.*
  buy the ticket.

Past participle constructions instead of adverbial clauses

- the past participle is used to express **a passive meaning**
  When the book is read by a professional actor, → *Read by a professional actor, the book sounds much better.*
  it sounds much better.

- the past participle can be **used as an adjective**
  a used car, mixed feelings, stonewashed jeans, a pleated dress, baked beans

Pairs of useful participial adjectives		
alarming – alarmed	depressing – depressed	frightening – frightened
amazing – amazed	disappointing – disappointed	interesting – interested
amusing – amused	disgusting – disgusted	relaxing – relaxed
annoying – annoyed	embarrassing – embarrassed	shocking – shocked
astonishing – astonished	exciting – excited	surprising – surprised
boring – bored	exhausting – exhausted	terrifying – terrified
confusing – confused	fascinating – fascinated	

 Be careful **not to mix up** these forms.
The book was boring. (active) **BUT** *Susan was really bored (from reading the book). (passive)*

Grammar and Language

Passive

tenses	active	passive
simple past	Paul Newman developed "Newman's Own" products.	"Newman's Own" products were developed by Paul Newman.
past progressive	England was accepting more immigrants at that time.	More immigrants were being accepted at that time by England.
past perfect	Lincoln's decree had freed the slaves before the war ended.	The slaves had been freed by Lincoln's decree before the war ended.
past perfect progressive	Owen had been watching Ben Hur until he fell asleep.	– not used –
simple present	The president gives an inaugural speech after being elected.	An inaugural speech is given by the president after being elected.
present progressive	An Asian-American is playing the role.	The role is being played by an Asian-American.
present perfect	Millions have crossed the border.	The border has been crossed by millions.
present perfect progressive	The reporters have been interviewing President Obama for hours.	– not used –
will-future	More CO_2 will cause increased global warming.	Increased global warming will be caused by more CO_2.
going to-future	The student is going to write an exam tomorrow.	An exam is going to be written by the student tomorrow.

Passive – usage

- to talk about a general truth or to make a general statement/announcement
  Something should be done to stop global warming.
  People are asked/requested not to smoke in this building.

- to emphasize the person/thing/animal being acted on
  Buffalo were almost wiped out in the 19th century.

- when writing in a scientific genre (research papers, scientific reports, descriptions of works of art)
  The acid was diluted with water and then filtrated into a glass container. After this, it was heated.

- to be vague about who is responsible
  Mistakes were made.

- when the agent of the action is irrelevant or unknown
  The painting was stolen from the Louvre last year.

You should NOT use the passive:
- when you have to be precise about who caused sth./who is responsible
- when you want to be precise and to the point (passive sentences can sound wordy and vague)

Sentences with two objects:

S	P	O	O
The teacher	explained	the rules	to the student.
The rules	were explained	to the student	by the teacher.
The student	was explained	the rules	by the teacher.
The woman	gave	him	an apple.
An apple	was given	to him	by the woman.
He	was given	an apple	by the woman.

When active is transformed into passive, pronouns in the object case have to be transformed into the subject case too:

me	→	I
him	→	he
her	→	she
us	→	we
them	→	they

Grammar and Language

Relative Clauses

There are two types of relative clauses, **defining relative clauses** and **non-defining relative clauses**.

1. Defining relative clauses

- are used to define a person or thing (in the main clause)

- a defining relative clause is **needed to understand what/who (exactly) is meant**; without it the information given in the main clause would be incomplete

- who, that and whose are used for people and which, that and whose for things
  Who was the girl who/that became pregnant?
  Juno is the girl whose baby is given up for adoption.
  The self-help group which/that wants to help obese people meets once a week.

- when that, who, which are objects of the relative clause they can be left out (= contact clause)
  The speech (which/that) the President gave was very inspiring.

- there is **no comma** between the defining relative clause and the main clause

- a preposition is preferably put at the end of the relative clause rather than at the beginning
  The apprenticeship (that) the girl was looking for had already been taken by someone else.

2. Non-defining relative clauses

- **give extra information** (that make a sentence more interesting); they **can be left out** without making the sentence incomprehensible

- who, whose are used for people and which, whose for things

- there are **commas** between the main clause and the non-defining relative clause to bracket (*einrahmen, einklammern*) the "non-essential" information.
  Owen Meany has always worked in the quarry, which is at the end of the road.

- you **cannot** use *that* in a non-defining relative clause

- in formal English, the preposition in the non-defining relative clause should be placed in front of who, which, whose; who is then changed to whom **after** a preposition
  Paul Newman, after whom Newman's Own was named, was well known for his charity work.

3. Participle constructions instead of defining relative clauses

- often participle constructions take the place of defining relative clauses when the relative pronoun is the subject of the relative clause

	S		present participle
The woman who adopts the baby is a nurse.	→	*The woman adopting the baby is a nurse.*

- participle constructions using the past participle have a passive meaning

	passive		
Two of the babies that were adopted were girls.	→	*Two of the babies adopted were girls.*

Grammar and Language

Grammar and Language

Tenses

past tenses	present tenses	future tenses

simple past
I worked.
	simple present
	I work./He works.
		future simple:
		– will-future
		   I will work.
		– going to-future
		   I am going to work./
		   He is going to work.

past progressive *I was working./We were working.*	present progressive *I am working./He is working.*	
past perfect *I had worked.*	present perfect *I have worked./He has worked.*	future perfect *I will have worked.*
past perfect progressive *I had been working.*	present perfect progressive *I have been working./* *He has been working.*	future perfect progressive *I will have been working.*
		simple present } with future present progressive } meaning

Simple present – usage

- for repeated actions (e. g. hobby, habit, daily event)
  Susan goes to band practice every Tuesday.
  Grandmother sends me a cake each Christmas.

- to express general truths, generalizations or scientific facts
  Independence Day is celebrated on July 4th.
  Water freezes at 0 degrees Celsius.

- for scheduled events in the near future
  The train leaves at 4.30.
  The store opens in 10 minutes.

- for states, i. e. non-progressive verbs (e. g. to want, to cost, to seem, to need, to owe, to own, to like, to mind, etc.)
  Susan seems to be eating too much chocolate; she has put on weight recently.
  Mr Miller owns two old houses in the neighbourhood.

- to talk or write about texts, works of art or to write a summary
  The exposition of the novel introduces the main characters, Michael and Elizabeth.
  The painting/sculpture represents Venus rising from the sea.

Present progressive – usage

- stresses the continuing nature of an act, event or condition
  Nora is reading the latest novel by Stephenie Meyer.
  CNN is broadcasting a speech given by the president.

- to describe a picture/cartoon (→ also in combination with simple present and often in the passive voice)
  In the foreground, a group of people can be seen sitting on a bench. They are laughing.

Present perfect and simple past – usage

simple past	present perfect
– a state, action or series of actions that was/were completed in the past *When Grandma was a child, she lived in France.* *In 1865, Abraham Lincoln was killed.* *Frank went into the study and wrote an email.*	– describes a state, action or series of actions that began in the past and continue(s) into the present *Lilly has dreamt about Brad Pitt every night this week.* – typically used to suggest that an action still has an effect on sth. in the present *The heat wave has lasted for three weeks.* (→ effect: now everything is dry)

Past progressive – usage

- for actions that were not complete at a past time
  At 8 o'clock, when Owen came home, Hester was reading.

past   ■   now →

- often used together with the simple past; the past progressive describes the longer action or situation and the simple past the shorter action that happened during the longer action
  While Juno was walking down the road she saw her friend.

    past progressive   **simple past**

- for actions that were taking place in the past at the same time (while)
  While the politicians were discussing the matter, the people were protesting violently.

Past perfect – usage

- when somebody is already talking about the past and wants to talk about an earlier time
  When Juno gave up her baby for adoption, she had already contacted the foster parents.

    simple past   **past perfect**

Past perfect progressive – usage

- for actions that had been going on for some time in the past before another action happened; to express the duration *(Dauer)* of an action or situation
  The people had already been waiting for an hour before the band finally started to play.

    past perfect progressive   **simple past**

Will-future and going to-future – usage

will-future	going to-future
– future facts/things we believe to be true *The president will support public service.* *I am certain you will get a good mark.* *I am sure you will like her.*	– if you are making a future prediction based on evidence in the present situation *Look at the traffic. We are not going to get there on time.* *Be careful! You are going to fall.*
– if you are not certain about the future; with expressions such as **probably, possibly, I think, I hope** *The climate summit will probably find a good solution.* *I hope the CO_2 emissions will be cut.*	
– at the very moment of making a decision *I will apply for the apprenticeship.* ⟶	– once you have made the decision *Tom, can you get me the address? I am going to write a CV and a letter of application.*

Grammar and Language

Narrative tenses

Narrative tenses are used when you want **to tell a story** or talk about situations or activities that happened at a defined past time. Do not mix past and present tenses when narrating past events – this will confuse the readers/listeners.

simple past

Everybody knew that Owen Meany did not drink.
Owen lit a cigarette and asked Hester for a dance.

past progressive

Owen and Hester were dancing closely when the teacher entered.
While they were dancing, the boys were laughing at them.

past perfect

We knew that Hester had been in love with the boatman from Tortola.

past perfect progressive

Owen and Hester had been dancing all night when the party finally ended.

Vocabulary and Phrases for Text Analysis

When you are asked to analyse and interpret a text, you should express yourself precisely and appropriately. Therefore, it is important to use a specific terminology that employs **technical terms** (e. g. stylistic devices) and a variety of formulations that make your text more fluent and less repetitive.

The following words and phrases are related to the most relevant aspects.

introduction	the author
<ul><li>The text deals with/is about …</li><li>The theme of the text is …</li><li>The text is composed of/consists of …</li><li>Three/two … different parts can be distinguished …</li><li>The first part runs from line … to line …</li><li>At the beginning of the text, …</li><li>The author begins by saying …</li><li>At the end of the text,/Finally,/Lastly, …</li><li>The first part forms the introduction …</li><li>The main/central/principal idea is …</li><li>In the conclusion, the author states that …</li><li>In the final part, the author …</li></ul>	<ul><li>The author thinks/says/believes that …</li><li>According to the author, …/In his/her view …</li><li>The author illustrates his/her point of view with …</li><li>The author makes a comment on …</li><li>The author is convinced that …</li><li>The author's judgments are (un)realistic/not objective/ unfounded/well-founded …</li><li>The reader can sympathize with the author's view on …</li><li>The author expresses doubts/questions …</li><li>The author makes remarks on …</li><li>The intention/aim/objective of the author is …</li><li>The author portrays believable characters.</li><li>The author gives a detailed/vague description of …</li></ul>
the text/plot/story	**the characters**
<ul><li>The story is told from the perspective of …</li><li>The plot is set in …</li><li>The text is written in an ironic tone.</li><li>The text contains comical elements.</li><li>The setting of the action is unreal/imaginary.</li><li>The action becomes more/less intense …</li><li>The situation seems quite absurd…</li><li>Suspense is created because/by …</li><li>The ending of the story is believable …</li></ul>	<ul><li>The main/principal character in the story is …</li><li>The author characterizes him/her as …</li><li>He has many positive traits …</li><li>His behaviour is marked by …</li><li>Another essential quality is …</li><li>She shows her superiority by saying that …</li><li>He is characterized as …</li><li>The protagonist lacks …</li><li>As far as his outward appearance is concerned, …</li><li>She plays an important/a secondary role …</li></ul>
the structure	**the action**
<ul><li>The exposition gives information about …</li><li>The first scene introduces …</li><li>The starting point for the action is …</li><li>The conflict reaches its climax in …</li><li>The turning point is indicated by …</li><li>The crisis is in scene …</li><li>In the last scene, …</li><li>This play/story has a happy/tragic ending.</li></ul>	<ul><li>The action takes place in …</li><li>The action develops in … stages …</li><li>The action progresses fast …</li><li>The scene contains a flashback.</li><li>The action is interrupted by …</li><li>This is one of the central scenes …</li><li>The development of the action is slowed down by …</li></ul>

Note: Explanations of the respective technical terms can be found in the Literary Terms section, pp. 135 ff.

Grammar and Language

Grammar and Language

purpose (of texts)	vocabulary
<ul><li>The author wants to arouse the reader's interest.</li><li>The text appeals to …</li><li>He/She tries to manipulate …</li><li>He/She wants the reader to become aware of …</li><li>The text addresses young/poor/… people …</li><li>It is the author's objective to create a feeling of …</li><li>The author attempts to influence the reader by …</li><li>The advert suggests to the reader that …</li></ul>	<ul><li>The vocabulary contains many colloquial expressions/ technical terms …</li><li>This word/term expresses fear …</li><li>This word has a negative meaning/negative associations …</li><li>This phrase suggests …</li><li>These phrases are examples of spoken language.</li><li>The choice of words gives the text its romantic/ technical/… character.</li><li>These expressions are typical of …</li></ul>
criticizing the author	**further useful expressions**
<ul><li>I (dis-)agree with the author on …</li><li>I do not understand why he/she …</li><li>I consider it to be wrong/difficult to …</li><li>This … cannot be taken seriously …</li><li>I would like to comment on …</li><li>It must be pointed out that …</li><li>This statement contradicts his/her view of …</li><li>There is a contradiction in …</li><li>It goes without saying that …</li><li>It is essential that …</li><li>This raises the question as to why he/she …</li><li>What really matters is …</li><li>This problem has nothing to do with …</li><li>This is of no importance/significance for …</li><li>As far as … is concerned, …</li><li>From this point of view, …</li><li>Generally speaking, …</li><li>As a matter of fact, …</li><li>In theory, …, but in reality, …</li></ul>	<ul><li>To give an explanation for …</li><li>The author pretends to know …</li><li>The author describes the characteristics of …</li><li>The article is based on …</li><li>The author makes an allusion to …</li><li>This sentence reveals the true character of …</li><li>He/She appeals to emotions rather than …</li><li>He/She quotes some experts as an example of …</li><li>The article relates … to …</li><li>The text conveys the impression that …</li><li>The writer establishes a relationship between …</li><li>The author's theses are …</li><li>He supports his thesis with …</li><li>Her outlook on life is …</li><li>He/She takes a positive/negative view of …</li><li>The author generalizes about …</li><li>This is a great simplification of …</li></ul>

→ When you analyse or interpret a text, you should use **Standard English**.

→ You should generally use the **present tense** when you describe, explain or analyse specific aspects of the text.

→ Be careful not to imitate the tone or the language of the text – when you write about a text written in colloquial English, you should still use Standard English in order to appear **impersonal and objective**.

→ Try to **vary the beginnings of your sentences** by employing different connectives.

→ Even when you express your personal opinion about a text/the author, etc., your choice of words should be appropriate and respectful. It can be helpful *not* to begin sentences with "I …" or "I think …" but to **focus on the text, the author**, etc. (e. g. *The article gives the impression that …, The author seems to intend to …*). This appears much more impersonal and academic.

→ **Do not overdo it by being too formal** or stilted – your text should reflect your view and stance on the matter.

→ Be careful **not to use short forms** (e. g. don't, doesn't, there's, haven't, you're, etc.) in the tasks that are related to the **comprehension, analysis and comment/evaluation** of texts. They should only be used in creative writing tasks, e. g. in an informal conversation, diary entry, or interior monologue, when you are asked to express your thoughts in a rather informal way. However, when you write e. g. a letter to the editor, you should use formal English.

Note: Explanations of the respective technical terms can be found in the Literary Terms section, pp. 135 ff.

Literary Terms

This glossary of literary terms is designed to help you understand the meaning of terms used in connection with literature or the analysis of literary texts.

Important terms marked with the asterisk symbol (*) throughout the Students' Book can be found here in thematic order.

Fiction/fictional texts

a) narrative texts (e. g. novel, short story, fable)

● **structure and plot**

allegory ['æləgəri]	a text that may be understood on a superficial or factual level and a deeper, more philosophical level; the characters are often personifications of abstract ideas (e. g. evil, love, etc.)
climax	the moment when the conflict is most intense
conflict	a struggle between different forces which produces suspense
dénouement [ˌdeɪˈnuːmã:] (resolution)	the final outcome, when the conflict is resolved
epigram	a short, witty statement which may be written in prose or verse
exposition	the very beginning of a fictional text which introduces the main character(s), the theme, the setting and the atmosphere
falling action	a reduction of suspense
flashback	an episode/event which interrupts the chronological order of a text and goes back in time to show what happened earlier
foreshadowing	hinting at later events
internal conflict	a struggle between two opposing views/values which takes place in a character's mind
(leit)motif ['laɪtməʊtiːf]	a theme/expression/object which recurs throughout the text and which refers to a certain person, situation or atmosphere
open ending	the conflict remains unresolved → the reader is left to reflect on possible resolutions
plot	the author's selection and structure of action as a set of events connected by cause and effect that are meant to create suspense
rising action	an increase in suspense
setting	place and time of a story/play
surprise ending	a sudden and unexpected turn of fortune/action
suspense	a feeling of tension/expectation
tension	the emotional strain caused by a conflict

● **narration**

acting time	the time from the beginning to the end of an episode in a text, this is usually longer than the narrating time because the writer can describe the passing of years in just a sentence; *erzählte Zeit*
interior monologue	a technique used within the stream of consciousness; a special kind of scenic presentation, often not in chronological order
mode of presentation – panoramic presentation – scenic presentation	the way the writer narrates events; *Darstellungsart* – the narrator tells the story as a condensed series of events, summarizing in a few sentences what happens over a longer period of time – the narrator shows an event in detail as it occurs, using dialogue, depicting thoughts and emotions, describing a scene, etc.

Grammar and Language

135

Grammar and Language

narrating time (= reading time)	the time it takes to relate an episode in a text (= reading time); it depends on the mode of presentation; *Erzählzeit*
narrator – omniscient [ɒmˈnɪsiənt] narrator – third-person narrator – first-person narrator – witness/observer narrator – objective/reliable – subjective/unreliable	person who tells the story (*not* the author!) – a narrator who seems to know everything – a narrator who stands outside the story and describes events in the third person – a narrator who is a character in a story; this is a limited point of view – a narrator who is a character in a story (protagonist or minor character) – a narrator who the reader can trust – a narrator who the reader is critical of
point of view/viewpoint – unlimited point of view – limited point of view	the perspective from which the characters, topics and events are presented (*not* the author!) – the reader can examine the action/characters from various angles – e. g. a first-person narrator who only has limited insight into the action/characters
stream of consciousness [ˈkɒnʃəsnəs]	the presentation of experience through the mind of one character in a text

b) drama (any work meant to be performed on stage or as a film)

act	the major division of a drama; an act consists of scenes
comedy	a drama which deals with a (light) topic in a more amusing way; it always has a happy ending
comic relief	a comic episode in a serious drama which aims at relieving tension by amusing the audience
dialogue	two or more people speaking to each other in a text
monologue	an extended speech by one character in a text; it might address other characters or the audience
one-act play	a short drama consisting of only one act
play	any dramatic work intended to be presented on stage, in film or on TV
scene	a subdivision in a drama
setting	the place and/or time in which an action takes place
short play	a short drama which takes about 30 minutes to perform
soliloquy [səˈlɪləkwi]	a speech delivered by a character alone on stage (used to reveal the character's thoughts, feelings or motives to the audience)
stage directions	a playwright's notes about how the drama is to be performed
tragedy	a drama in which the protagonist undergoes a series of misfortunes until he or she finally falls; the hero(ine) has to experience a reversal of fortune, i. e. from happiness to misery

● **characters**

antagonist	the opponent of the protagonist
anti-hero(ine)	a protagonist who does not have the qualities of a typical hero, and is either more like an ordinary person or is morally bad and does not fit into society
characterization – direct characterization – indirect characterization	the way of presenting a character in a text – the narrator or another character describes the character; alternatively, the character may describe him- or herself – the reader/audience learns about the character through action and dialogue
flat character	a minor character who does not develop in the course of the action
hero(ine) [ˈhɪərəʊ; ˈherəʊɪn]	the principal male or female character in a drama; he/she is usually in conflict with another character, fate and/or society
minor character	a character of less importance for the course of the action

protagonist (= main character)	the main character in a drama/play
round character	a character who develops in the course of action and therefore has the ability to change

c) poetry (literature that has a certain pattern, such as rhyme, rhythm, sentence structure)

anapaest [ˈænəpiːst]	metrical foot of three syllables (unstressed – unstressed – stressed): e. g. *underneath* _ _ ' _
concrete poem	a type of poem in which the words form a shape or picture
connotation	additional meaning of a word beyond its dictionary definition, for example, due to the associations that are formed through personal experience
dactyl [ˈdæktɪl]	metrical foot of three syllables (stressed – unstressed – unstressed): e. g. *merrily* ' _ _ _
denotation	the actual definition of a word (its dictionary definition)
end rhyme	a rhyme at the end of two lines
enjambement [ɪnˈdʒæmbmənt] (= run-on line)	a sentence which runs from one line to another without a pause/break
foot	a group of stressed and unstressed syllables within a line of poetry which forms a metrical unit
free verse	a poem written without a particular rhyme scheme or regular metre
iamb [ˈaɪæm(b)]	metrical foot of two syllables (unstressed – stressed) e. g. *become* _ ' _
imagery [ˈɪmɪdʒəri]	term for the use of images created by words that are used to appeal to the reader's imagination → often metaphors and/or similes
line	a structural unit in a poem; it is usually classified by a certain number of feet
metre	the regular rhythmic patterns of a poem/the arrangement of words according to stressed and unstressed syllables
poem	a composition which contains a structured line sequence and a special arrangement of words, a special rhythm, the use of imagery
rhyme	using words that repeat syllable sounds
rhyme scheme [skiːm] – rhyming couplets – alternate rhyme – embracing rhyme	the arrangement of rhymes in a poem – two consecutive lines with the same rhyme: aa bb – lines with the rhyme scheme: ab ab – lines with the rhyme scheme: abba
rhythm	the arrangement of stressed or unstressed syllables in writing
sonnet [ˈsɒnɪt] – quatrain – couplet	poem consisting of 14 lines, usually written in iambic pentameter; e. g. the Shake-speare-an sonnet consists of three quatrains and a couplet with the rhyme scheme abab cdcd efef gg – a stanza of four lines (e. g. in a sonnet) – two successive rhyming lines (e. g. at the end of a sonnet)
speaker	the fictional person who is imagined as saying the text of a poem (*not* identical with the poet!)
stanza	a major division in a poem consisting of several lines
trochee [ˈtrəʊkiː]	metrical foot of two syllables (stressed – unstressed) e. g. *happen* ' _ _
verse	a stanza in a poem or song; poetry written in metre

Grammar and Language

137

d) lyrics/songs (in addition to the aspects mentioned under *poetry*, also consider these devices)

genre of music	a particular type or style of music, e.g. Jazz, Rap, Funk, Heavy Metal, Protest Song, etc.
instrumentation	selection and combination of the musical instruments that are used in a song, e.g. electronic instruments, percussion, violin, etc.
onomatopoeia [ˌɒnəˌmætəˈpiːə]	words that imitate a sound associated with the thing being named, e.g. buzz, cuckoo, hum, etc.
registers of English	the words, style and grammar used, e.g. poetic, formal, slang, non-standard, in order to express a certain message or set of values
rhythm, beat	the regular pattern of long and short notes in music
vocals	the part of a piece of music that is sung, for example, by a lead singer, a choir, etc.

Non-fiction/non-fictional texts

● **text type**

argumentation	an argumentative text deals with ideas and/or controversy; it expresses a clear opinion and gives reasons/arguments to support it
description	a descriptive text aims at describing things/developments, etc.
exposition	in an expository text, the writer explains a rather complex problem in a precise and objective way
instruction	an instructive text gives advice about a particular matter; it typically includes commands and recommendations

● **text form**

comment	a kind of argumentation in which the writer/speaker gives his or her opinion on a certain topic
editorial	a comment, usually written by the chief editor, that gives his or her opinion on a certain topic of common interest
essay (= literary appreciation)	a text in which the writer expresses his or her personal views on a certain topic; it usually follows a certain compositional pattern, i.e. the use of unity and balance (= statement – development – conclusion)
feature story	a report written to arouse human interest, typically by concentrating on an individual case that many readers can identify with
interview	a dialogue in which someone, usually a journalist, asks another person questions on a topic of common interest; may appear in a newspaper, on TV, etc.
leader/leading article	the most important or prominent news story in a magazine/newspaper
letter to the editor	a letter written by a reader to the editor of a magazine/newspaper in order to express a personal opinion on some topic (→ comment)
news story	a report based on facts and background information that deals with a topical event that the public is interested in
report	a text that aims at answering the "five w's": who?, what?, when?, where? and why?, which can be checked and verified by the reader
review	a short critical evaluation of a work of art (literature, film, etc.)
scientific report	a text written for scientific purposes, usually containing many technical terms (→ report)
sermon	a religious discourse delivered as part of a church service
speech – political speech – laudatory [ˈlɔːdətəri] speech	a formal talk or an address delivered to an audience – an address delivered for a political purpose, e.g. the inaugural address of a president or a crisis speech – a speech delivered in order to express praise, e.g. when sb. is awarded a prize

• structural devices

column ['kɒləm]	*Textspalte*; mostly used in newspapers and magazines
conclusion	the main idea is often re-stated here or the main aspects of the text may be recapped (*kurz zusammenfassen*) in summary
heading/headline	a caption that is written above a text to arouse the reader's interest
introduction	lead-in to the topic, often by referring to the "five w's" in order to attract the reader's interest and lure him or her into the story
line of argument(ation)	the way different reasons are gradually developed and structured to convince a reader of a particular point of view (→ train of thought)
main part	the part of the text in which the writer demonstrates a topic/explains his or her intention/discusses a topic or problem, etc.
paragraph	a division of a text dealing with a particular idea that begins on a new line
passage	a short extract from a text that may consist of several paragraphs
subheading	a caption that subdivides a text into logical sections
theme/topic/subject	a central idea in a text which binds all of its elements together
train of thought	the way a series of ideas is gradually developed and structured

• rhetorical/stylistic devices

alliteration	the repetition of a sound, usually a consonant, at the beginning of neighbouring words
allusion	indirect reference to a famous event, person or piece of literature
anaphora [əˈnæfərə]	successive sentences starting with the same word
antithesis [ænˈtɪθəsɪs]	contrast; opposing words, phrases, views, characters, etc.
choice of words	the decision to use a particular word based on such aspects as style, register, connotation, etc.
ellipsis [iˈlɪpsɪs]; ellipses (*pl.*)	a situation in which words are left out in a sentence but the sentence can still be understood; ellipses are often used by poets or authors to compress and intensify certain ideas/thoughts
euphemism [ˈjuːfəmɪzəm]	using polite expressions for sth. unpleasant
exaggeration/hyperbole [haɪˈpɜːbəli]	making sth./sb. sound better, more exciting, dangerous, etc. than in reality
image	a word intended to appeal to the reader's imagination and to bring a new perception to an object (→ figurative language, e.g. metaphors, similes)
irony	saying the opposite of what you mean
(leit)motif	a theme, expression or object which recurs throughout a text and which refers to a certain person, situation or atmosphere
manner of speaking	a style that is typical of a particular person, e.g. politician or worker, etc.
metaphor [ˈmetəfə(r)]	poetic comparison without using *like* or *as* (e.g. an ocean of love)
paradox	seeming impossible at first glance but recognized as true on second thought
parallelism	repeating similar or identical words/phrases in neighbouring lines/sentences/paragraphs
personification	presenting ideas/objects/animals as persons (e.g. a smiling moon)
pun	a play on words
reference	a connection to sth. else (→ allusion)
register/level of speech	the words, style and grammar used, e.g. formal/informal English, colloquialisms, slang, non-standard English, etc.; such aspects are typically adjusted according to the addressees
repetition	deliberately using a word/phrase more than once

Grammar and Language

rhetorical question	question to which the answer is obvious or to which no answer is possible/expected
simile ['sɪməli]	comparison using *like* or *as*
symbol	sth. concrete (object, character, event) standing for sth. abstract (cross – Christianity; horseshoe – luck)
syntax ['sɪntæks] – hypotactical structure – paratactical structure	arrangement of words in a phrase/sentence/text – rather complicated and long sentences, involving sub-clauses – a rather simple sentence structure, mostly consisting of main clauses, sometimes connected with the conjunctions *and, or*
tone	the manner or mood, e. g. macabre, optimistic, etc.

The media

agony aunt/uncle	a person who writes for a newspaper or magazine giving advice in reply to people's letters about their personal problems
feature story/human interest	a story or part of a story in a newspaper that people find interesting because it describes the feelings, experiences, etc. of the people involved
front page – cover story – special feature – leading article/editorial	the first page of a newspaper where the most important news is printed – the main story in a magazine that goes with the picture shown on the front cover – a special article or report on sb./sth. (*Sonderbeitrag*) – an important article in a newspaper that expresses the editor's opinion about a news item or a particular issue
headline	the title of a newspaper article printed in large letters, especially at the top of the front page
Internet – blog – chatroom – website – web forum	an international computer network connecting other networks and computers – a personal record that sb. puts on their website giving an account of their activities and their opinions, and discussing other sites on the Internet, events, etc. – a site on the Internet where people can communicate with each other in real time – a set of interconnected webpages, generally located on the same server, and prepared and maintained by a person, group or organization – a site on the Internet where people can exchange opinions and ideas on a particular issue
letter to the editor	a (mostly critical) letter written by the reader of a newspaper/magazine in response to an article or a story
masthead ['maːsthed]	– the name of the newspaper at the top of the front page – the part of a newspaper or a news website which gives details about the people who work on it or other information about it
television/radio – broadcasting company/ corporation – channel – programme – commercial (break) – documentary [ˌdɒkjuˈmentri] – factual report – feature film – live coverage – soap (opera)	 – a company whose business is to make and transmit radio and TV programmes – a television station (*Programm*) – sth. that you watch on TV or listen to on the radio (*Sendung*) – an advertisement on the radio or on television – a film, radio or television programme giving facts about something – a report based on facts (*Tatsachenbericht*) – *Spielfilm* – sth. broadcast/sent while the event is actually happening, not pre-recorded (*Direktübertragung*) – a story about the life and problems of a group of fictional people that is broadcast every day or several times a week on TV or radio

the press	
– quality newspapers/ broadsheets	– usually larger formats that have in-depth articles and present facts that are based on serious research
– tabloids/popular newspapers	– usually smaller formats that are more sensationalist
– magazines/periodicals	– periodical publications financed by advertising; printed in colour on quality paper

Films/movies

documentary (film)	a film, television or radio programme that gives detailed factual information about a particular subject
docusoap	a supposedly unscripted television programme that shows what happens in the daily life of real people (= reality TV)
feature film	a full-length film that has a story, which is acted out by professional actors, and is usually shown in a cinema (*Spielfilm*)
screenplay/script – shooting script	the words that are written down for actors to say in a film, and the instructions that tell them what they should do – a script with additional information/details given by the director (e. g. drafts, technical details, arrows to indicate how to move the camera, etc.)
slug lines	numbered lines between the dialogue lines that indicate a change in location and time (e. g. INT, EXT); each slug line begins a new scene
storyboard	a graphic organizer that displays images in sequence (like a picture story) in order to help the film crew to know where the cameras are to be positioned or where/how a character has to stand/move, etc.

Grammar and Language

Grammar Exercise Finder (in alphabetical order)

Grammar/Language	Text/Skill No.
adjectives/adverbs	4 9 12 16
adverbial clauses	14
collocations	10
formal vs. informal English	15 18
gerund	6 18
if-clauses (conditional sentences)	3 9 16 18
indirect speech (reported speech)	1 7
language practice	6 13 18
modals/modal auxiliaries	3 5
(replacing) overused words	15
paraphrasing	1 9
participle constructions	6 11 18
passive	9 18
questions	5
relative clauses (defining/non-defining)	11
sentence adverbials	14
synonyms (or antonyms)	8 17
tenses	1 2 4 7
future tenses	2
vocab training	17

Acknowledgements

|alamy images, Abingdon/Oxfordshire: Awakening/ Padovani, Simone 12; Bell, Brendan / Courtesy of Pest Control Office, Banksy, London, 2012 57; Bourdillon, Mark 57; Dwyer, Michael 36; frans lemmens 27; Lifestyle pictures 27; Oeian, Liv 15. |Andrews McMeel Syndication, Kansas City, MO: STAHLER ©2013 Jeff Stahler. Reprinted by permission of ANDREWS MCMEEL SYNDICATION for UFS. All rights reserved. 50. |Art Explosion, Calabasas, CA: 118, 118. |Axel Springer Syndication GmbH, Berlin: Infografik WELT-online vom 9.3.2019 45, 46. |Berghahn, Matthias, Bielefeld: 20, 29, 77. |Cagle Cartoons, Santa Barbara, CA: Koterba, Jeff 76; Sack, Steve 87; Weyant, Christopher 34. |Cartoon Movement, Amsterdam: Osval 51; Popa Matumula 74. |CartoonStock.com, Bath: Mello, Silvano 65; Spaulding, Trevor 65; Tugg 50. |Domke, Franz-Josef, Hannover: 53, 79, 91, 92, 97, 112. |End Now Foundation, Hyderabad: Anil Rachamalla 70, 70, 70, 70. |FOCUS Magazin Verlag GmbH, München: FOCUS 18/2019 66, 67, 67. |Getty Images, München: Spatari, Alexander 101. |Globe Cartoon, Geneva: © Chappatte in NZZ am Sonntag, Zurich 58, 96. |Guardian News & Media Limited, London: 2019 112. |Hawkins, Ed: 72, 72. |HUD Exchange, Washington: The U.S. Department of Housing and Urban Development: The 2018 Annual Homelessness Assessment Report (AHAR) to Congress 40, 40. |iStockphoto.com, Calgary: Alliya23 54. |Kratzer, Max, Oberschleißheim: 60. |Ocean. Now!, Berlin: 95; Photo: Saskia Uppenkamp 95, 95. |Picture-Alliance GmbH, Frankfurt/M.: ANP/van Weel, Koen 47; AP Photo/Getty Images/Moore, John 98. |Plaßmann, Thomas, Essen: 14. |Save the Children Deutschland e.V., Berlin: Talitha Brauer 18. |SPIEGEL-Verlag Rudolf Augstein GmbH & Co. KG, Hamburg: DER SPIEGEL 83, 84; Der SPIEGEL 84; DER SPIEGEL 29/2019 82. |Stutte, Matthias, Krefeld: 89. |Stuttmann, Klaus, Berlin: 14, 22. |WWF Deutschland, Berlin: 73.

Wir arbeiten sehr sorgfältig daran, für alle verwendeten Abbildungen die Rechteinhaberinnen und Rechteinhaber zu ermitteln. Sollte uns dies im Einzelfall nicht vollständig gelungen sein, werden berechtigte Ansprüche selbstverständlich im Rahmen der üblichen Vereinbarungen abgegolten.